Speak ...
Shantae W...
12-17-17

The First

Lady

For Harry
You made this particular journey easy.

For Nia and Kai
May you discover, know, and always use your authentic voice.

The First

Lady

*African American Pastors' Wives
in Their Own Voices*

Dr. Shauntae Brown White

Acknowledgements

This project has been nearly 15 years in the making, and I have met a lot of people along the journey who contributed to its birth. Though 19 are featured, I interviewed over 30 pastors' wives. Everyone has a story to tell, and every story has value. From poor recording technology at the beginning of the project to choosing not to share her story, several women who were interviewed are not featured. Yet, I appreciate the time each woman gave me.

Marilyn Anderson (Cincinnati, Ohio) Stephanie Carter (Dallas, Texas) Lisa Harvin (Baltimore, Maryland) Twanna Henderson (Matthews, North Carolina) Cynthia Martin (Dallas, Texas) Sharon Moore (Upper Marlboro, Maryland) Edna Ruff (Kansas City, Missouri) Gail Smiley (Hamilton, Ohio) Diane Smiley (Hamilton, Ohio) Stephanie Thomas (Baltimore, Maryland) Altamese Y. Williams (Capitol Heights, Maryland) Mattie Watson (Kansas City, Missouri)

There are many people who helped me talk through my ideas over the years—too many to name. However, a few people stand out. Kathi Brown, Sharnine Herbert, Marsha Jackson, Regina Robinson, Gwen Etter-Lewis, Rhonda Smith, and Patricia Thomas were always willing to listen to me formulate my ideas and/or encouraged me to complete and publish the project.

I met Johnny Stephens when I was shopping the proposal for a publisher. He was one of only a few acquisition editors who got and understood the project. Thank you for believing in it and in me.

After going through several versions of the book cover, the question was raised, "Why don't you be on your own cover?" Initially,

4

I was reluctant. Once, I decided to go ahead, there were several people who helped the moving parts fall into place: Krika Bradsher (Sophia's Sunflower Salon) is THE best natural hair stylist and always seems to manage to "get me in" when I absolutely need it. From the time I watched Dajaun Jones (In His Image Photography) patiently work with each dancer and parent during a photo session for my older daughter's dance recital many years ago, I made a note that I wanted to work with him. I am so glad he was available on short notice. Many thanks to Rhonda Raney and Susie Sanders for loaned items. Many thanks to Ken Strickland! I am glad we got to work together again on another book cover. I appreciate your patience to work with someone who kind of sort of knows what she wants but won't know it until she sees it.

My number one cheerleader is my husband, Harry. He is also always the first person who helps me think through anything and acts as my first editor, whether he feels like it at the time or not. He has made being a pastor's wife easy, all the while encouraging me to be my best self, reach my full potential, and not only fly but fly high.

My girls, Nia and Kai, help keep me balanced. Thank you for always being excited about whatever I am doing. They were happy to serve as my stylists for the book cover photo shoot, which actually made it fun.

ISBN: 978-0-9907598-4-3

HERITAGE PUBLISHING
1261 Andrew Donelson, Hemitage TN.

Table of Contents

Forward

Rev. Stephanie Buckhanon Crowder, Ph.D.
Park Manor Christian Church
Chicago, IL

"She is not just the first lady. She is the only lady. To be first implies there is a second." I admit I felt myself sliding under the pew when I heard a man say this. Perhaps in his own way he was trying to honor the position of the pastor's wife. It could also have been a warning to potential suitors that this first lady was off-limits. I think the comment also speaks to the ambiguous nature of the first lady in the church. People are not always so sure what to say about her or to her or how to approach her. She is not the pastor, but she comes with his "packaged presentation." Hers is not the task of paid spiritual leader; yet, the onus of the women's and/ or children's ministries often falls on her uncompensated shoulders. No, she—we—are not the Proverbs 31 woman. However, our proverbial presence is the source of wonder and bewilderment. (You think former FLOTUS Michelle Obama had to wrestle with this? Yet, I digress.)

What people do not realize is that even the first lady herself experiences discord. There is the drama of having to filter snide comments, eye-rolling, and other microaggressions from the saints. Unknown to the congregation is that the pastor's beloved also has her own internal strife. She, too, wrestles with the ambiguity of being both/and, either/or, here and there. While trying to manage public presentation and performance, the first lady must emotionally multitask her own anger, fears, frustration and just simple exhaustion. If she is a momma/first lady, there is an added layer of responsibility in caring for and protecting the first children. A first lady working outside of the home is another stream flowing into these ecclesial waters. Who can she talk to about her internal conundrum?

This work provides the space for the first lady, many first ladies, to talk it through and tell their stories. Dr. Shauntae Brown White boldly gathers an eclectic group of first ladies who dare to speak their truth. The First Lady is a compilation of voices representing various denominations, geographical locales, congregational sizes, educational backgrounds, and professional standings. What ties these women together is the common thread in the title first lady. Yet, the narratives are unique, and each woman dares the reader to go behind the curtain. From Shauntae White's openness of the harrowing experience about her hair to Judith Hayes Davis and Dianne Cleaver reflecting on just being married to men, we are immediately invited to get beyond all the first lady pomp and circumstance.

Vanessa Oliver Ward shifts this work from first lady to first lady/co-pastor. Her heartfelt story reveals how she covers her family and the church during her husband's illness. The world of the first children comes to bear through Andrea Hayles and many of the essays. These mothers help us to see that even the pastor's sons and daughters must live, move, and have their being under the congregation's microscope. Such a lens is difficult for an adult introvert, as Wanda Taylor-Smith and fellow contributors aver. The first lady is compelled, let's say, conscripted to show up, dressed to the nines, when she longs to dwell inside with a book and a glass of wine. These stories, while personal, do not mince

10

words about the challenges surrounding and the need to establish first family boundaries.

I did something you are never to do in the church—I called names. I mentioned a few of the testimonies here not to establish any hierarchy, but to show that the role of first lady is not homogeneous. It is as different as the women presented here. The tasks, talents, and truths of each of these women is as unique as their embodiment of the title first lady.

While reading this work, I found myself revisiting my own working momma/first lady journey. Although my story is not included, in many ways it is represented. Juggling children, my own call to ministry, and congregational expectations can be overwhelming. The First Lady provided oxygen so that I could breathe a little easier. I am not the only one. We are not alone. This work assures us that while we are the first lady, we are not the first woman ever in this role. The power lies not in revealing our business, but in telling our story.

From one first lady to many first ladies, thank you. Here's to

#FirstLadyMagic!

Introduction

"The Pastor's Wife: A Peculiar Situation"

In 1998, I experienced several life-changing events. First, I married a Christian minister, which meant changing my religious denomination and joining a new church. Second, I moved to another city, leaving family and friends. I went from being an active layperson in the congregation where I grew up and people knew my name to being Reverend White's wife, or the term commonly used in the black church, the *first lady*.

I had my epiphany at Christmas when the Sunday school children made bookmarks as Christmas gifts. My husband's bookmark was addressed, "To Pastor White." Mine was addressed, "To Pastor Wife." That gift made me chuckle, and it also painted a vivid picture of one of the biggest challenges I would face: defining my role as a first lady.

So, there I was in a new city, with a new husband, at a new church, trying to find my place. This was my husband's first job as a pastor and my first time as a pastor's wife. Fortunately, we were blessed with a congregation that was overwhelmingly warm and welcoming to us. Some of the women did their best to include me in activities, and most people treated me with the same respect they gave my husband. There was one aspect of my new role that I did not like: some people's fascination with the details of my personal life.

There was a small circle of women who were extremely curious about me and what went on in our house and were bold enough to ask: "How much is the rent in your apartment complex?" Of my job search and prospects of employment: "Are you looking for a job hard enough?" "Are you just laying low and keeping cool and watching TV all day?" There was a preoccupation with whether I could cook: "Do you know how to cook?" "Do you cook?" "Pastor White is over there, and she doesn't cook for him."

After I had my first child, there was a discussion about if I was maternal. While I established my own boundaries with these women and controlled the information I wanted them to have, I secretly longed for the opportunity to say just once, "Mind your own damn business!" But the pastor's wife isn't supposed to say that, right?

Fortunately, I was at a place in my life where I was comfortable with myself. And, as time progressed and I matured in my walk with the Lord, I realized that while some comments might be annoying, disturbing, and even hurtful, the calling on my life to participate in Christian ministry and be a help-meet to my husband as he brought people to Christ was more significant than what others had to say about me because it was not all about me.

God also gave me eyes of compassion. At some time in our lives, most of us have struggled with the fleshly desire to participate in gossip or analyze the shortcomings of others. Hopefully, as we develop in our faith walk, that desire decreases or is quenched all together. God allowed me to see, clearly and without judgment, that the women who were preoccupied with my life and shortcomings were unfulfilled in their own lives. With that revelation, I was able to move from being cordial and distant to softening my interaction with these invasive women. I got to know some of the women and their life stories, which confirmed God's revelation.

Being a pastor's wife has challenged me to stretch. I can't say that I always master the lesson, but it was clear that God was calling me to demonstrate the same love that he shows us. In spite of our shortcomings, our moodiness, our selfishness, and all of our fleshliness, God still loves us and demonstrates that love.

Intrusive people are but one of the trials of being married to the pastor. Likewise, there are also many things to celebrate about the role of first lady. Among them is the support you receive if you are fortunate enough to serve in a warm and loving church. This was especially important to me as we began to have children in a city where we had no family.

I was overwhelmed when our first daughter, Nia, was born, and the women gave me the shower of the century. While we received an abundance of material things, and there was very little we had to purchase ourselves, I was more moved by the love that was expressed in the gift-giving and the excitement shared about the birth of our first child.

I am appreciative that the women organized a schedule that supplied us with meals for the first three weeks after we came home with our baby. The support of sisterhood did not stop there. I am thankful for Annie Rivers who volunteered to watch my daughter my first week back to work when my mother, who unexpectedly had surgery, could not travel and my husband was out of town. I will be forever grateful to Sue Fambrough, who babysat Nia as if she were her own grandchild from the time she was five months old. And I thank Regina Robinson for my "five minutes of peace" during church service when she would take Nia to sit with her.

These are just a few of the countless examples of how our first church showered us with love. I believe that after eight years of my husband serving there, many of the women moved past respecting and relating to me as a position and embraced me as a person.

Being married to the pastor puts his wife in a peculiar situation. In few other jobs is a wife so aware of and can observe her husband's performance, and, perhaps, even be involved in his vocation. A lawyer, doctor, or construction worker's wife is rarely in the courtroom, operating room, or at the construction site. The majority of the knowledge these wives have of their husbands' experiences on their jobs is by what they tell them.

As pastors' wives, some of us put in "sweat equity" at our husband's place of employment by being actively involved in the life of the ministry. We have to learn and pray for discernment of when to bring something to his attention and when to leave it alone. Sometimes, we must listen to criticism about our husband. Moreover, in this peculiar situation, we are part of a community that by its very nature encourages fellowshipping with others within the church, which often leads to developing intimacy with other believers.

If one is an active layperson, we learn about the trials, struggles, grief, and joys of other believers through our participation in ministries, Bible studies, prayer groups, and other opportunities for fellowship. However, as a pastor's wife, you can share some of those experiences, but there are boundaries you establish and precautions you take to keep your private life private.

As a single, young adult layperson not married to the pastor, many people from my church became part of my social network. I talked to them throughout the week, and on the weekend, I socialized with the same people with whom I worshiped on Sunday. On the contrary, as a pastor's wife, in a new city, though I wanted to be warm and friendly to everyone, the church is the last place where I tried to find friendship.

In fact, I have always been intentional about establishing a social network outside of the church for two primary reasons: (1) I decided early on I needed a life outside of the church, as did my husband. We both knew we needed something else to talk about when we were to together. (2) Not everyone can handle a friendship with the pastor or his wife. Although a pastor is used by God to lead a congregation, he or she is still plagued with human frailties and foibles. This is something that most healthy pastors and wives do not try to hide; however, not every congregant is spiritually mature or emotionally balanced to witness this humanity at an intimate level. When my husband first started pastoring, an older pastor's wife in the city said to me, "Pray that God raise up one good friend for you." Fortunately, He did both in and out of the church.

There are many joys to being a pastor's wife. Among them, watching the transformation of people's lives; watching God use your husband; having the opportunity to be a mentor to women; and, if correctly used, providing leadership to a ministry. There are also many challenges: listening to criticism about yourself, your husband, or your children; living in the proverbial fishbowl; and having to share your husband with a congregation of people when it is not always convenient for your family life.

After nearly 20 years of marriage and ministry, I have developed three goals for myself: (1) to continue my own spiritual growth and development in the Lord; (2) to have a healthy and realistic appraisal of the church and the people who make up the body and to help my husband do the same; (3) to instill a thirst for the knowledge and things of God in my children and nurture a spiritually whole family. Whether I am dealing with the challenges or the treasures, I, like so many other pastors' wives, had to figure out how to negotiate the performance of the role while honoring and glorifying God, representing my husband, and being true to myself.

Beyond the role of first lady in the African American church are individual women whose experiences are diverse and transcend traditional stereotypes. I wanted to discover how other pastor's wives have managed this role. While I am sure that all pastors' wives share similar experiences, I have chosen to focus on African American women.

One aspect that must be considered is the role of the black church in the African American community. The black church has played a pivotal role in shaping the history and experiences of African Americans in the United States. The church has been the primary spiritual, social, cultural, as well as the most autonomous institution in the African American community. Unlike its white counterpart, the African American church has taken on multiple roles and burdens that have exceeded addressing the spiritual life of its members.

Consequently, the leader, the African American pastor, is often considered a prominent and esteemed community leader. While there are certainly negative connotations and stereotypes of African American pastors, more often than not, they experience reverence and sometimes notoriety. Quite naturally, his spouse is subject to the respect and the notoriety of her husband.

This is a collection of the narratives of 19 pastors' wives and widows primarily from the East, the South, and the Midwest. These women vary in age ranging from 30 to 70-plus and represent five different denominations, including Baptist; African Methodist Episcopal (AME); African Methodist Episcopal Zion (AMEZ); the Church of God in Christ (COGIC); Pentecostal Assemblies of the World (PAW); the only predominantly white denomination, The United Methodist Church (UMC); and non-denominational affiliations.

The size of the church where their husbands currently serve or formerly served range from 50 members to megachurches with over 2,000 members. African American women are diverse in our experiences, and pastors' wives are no different. From dentists and educators to social workers and lawyers, this remarkable group of women collectively have a wealth of formal education among them. While this shows the diversity of pastors' wives and African American women, it by no means devalues the stories and experiences of women who do not have the same educational backgrounds and who, unfortunately, are not equally represented in this collection of narratives.

While the women share similar, yet unique experiences, it was clear that each woman had something vital to say. And at the end of the interviews, many women expressed a feeling of catharsis.

For me, this project is a labor of love. In working with this group of remarkable women, I learned something from every woman I interviewed. They didn't know it, but they offered me words of wisdom and encouragement. I felt their pain as they shared theirs of being criticized, fighting to get out of the proverbial box, or being betrayed. We also laughed at the things that only a pastor's wife could understand.

When I prepared to edit their stories, I thanked God for entrusting me with them and continually prayed that I would do them justice.

My prayer is that these stories touch the reader as much as they have touched me and that other pastors' wives can see their experiences in these women's stories and know that they are not alone. It is also my prayer that our husbands and congregants better understand our peculiar situations.

Finally, it is my hope that parishioners understand that we are real people, with real feelings, suffering the same hurts and pains of life as they do. We are wives who want to protect and encourage our husbands as they lead vital congregations and fulfill their calling. We are mothers who want to protect our children from being scarred by mean church people or those who have unrealistic expectations of them. We are women of God striving to glorify Him. We are not perfect. We struggle with the same issues of the flesh (taming our tongue, self-control, love, kindness, for example) just as many of our congregants do.

Of course, this book cannot tell the whole story for each woman. In fact, what is captured here is a snapshot of each woman's experiences. I interviewed these women over a course of five years beginning in 2004. Then the manuscript sat for several years because I couldn't find a publisher and demands from my own life and responsibilities made little time to push this to fruition.

For some of the women, the situations they shared have changed. We all have changed. These narratives reflect where the women were at that time. Yet, these experiences and reflections from more than ten years ago help to shape who we are today. The interview date and the church where her husband served at the time is noted in each narrative to help provide context. Hopefully, through the diverse experiences of these 19 women, we can create a composite of the pastor's wife that is more realistic, authentic, and human.

CHAPTER 2

SHAUNTAE BROWN WHITE
Married to the Rev. Dr. Harry L. White, Jr.
Watts Chapel Missionary Baptist Church
Raleigh, NC

"I am not just a church member, and finding the delicate balance between being a faithful member and wife to the pastor is sometimes challenging."

My husband and I have had the fortunate experience of being able to grow together as we figured out how the church and ministry fit into our lives, marriage, and family. Both of us have evolved and changed over the journey. We were engaged when he was called to pastor his first church. He began pastoring on May 1, and we got married May 30 of the same year. That year was full of new and exciting transitions. We were moving to a new city and trying to discover how to be husband and wife as well as pastor and pastor's wife. I was also trying to find my way professionally.

At the time, I was a doctoral student who was ABD (all but dissertation). Much to my mother's displeasure, I not only got married before I graduated, but I also moved away from my program. A rule of thumb in academia is to stay in the physical locale of your doctorate program until you complete your degree or run the risk of never finishing. I always knew that I would finish, but for 18 months, I never touched my dissertation. To my mother, her greatest fear seemed apparent: I would never finish my Ph.D.

A few months after we had been married, my mother said, "Just remember you have your own gifts and talents, too. You are a star in your own right." Because the completion of my degree had caused such a strain on our relationship, I am not sure that I received what she was saying at the time. In hindsight, after I became a mother of daughters, I realized she was speaking of more than just the degree. It was about Shauntae holistically reaching her full potential as a life partner, a help-meet for Harry, and as a woman. I believe the majority of married women have this dilemma at some point, but it's especially true of women married to men who are public figures.

In the early years, people would always ask me, "What's it like to be a first lady?" My answer was always, "It's much easier than being married." Anyone who has been married knows that a healthy, holistic marriage takes a tremendous amount of work, especially in the early years while you are trying to navigate the marital terrain.

From the beginning, the role of pastor's wife was simple. I attribute that to two things. Even at the age of 27, when I got married, by God's grace, I was in a place in my life where I was confident and secure with myself. Equally important, I married a man who believed he did not need a pastor's wife, he needed a wife. He gave me the freedom to be me and to define the role of pastor's wife in my own way.

Concerning church, my husband expected me to fulfill my role as a member: Attend church on a regular basis—and that didn't mean every time the doors opened. Tithe. Be active in a ministry. Be committed to nurturing my own spiritual growth. All he expected me to be was a faithful member. But I was not just a member, and finding the delicate balance between being a faithful church member and a wife to the pastor was sometimes challenging. It would take several years before I really understood what my husband needed me to be.

I have never considered being a pastor's wife as my identity; I see it as one of the many roles I perform. I am a wife and mother, foremost. I am a daughter, niece, cousin, and friend. I have a career. I am a professor and scholar. I am active at my girls' school. While I do not use the term *first lady* to self-identify, I do not correct someone who refers to me as such. It's never bothered me when people introduce me by simply saying, "This is our pastor's wife." Yes, I do have a name and an identity, but in that context, to many congregants, that is who I am, and that's acceptable to me. The titles *pastor's wife* or *first lady* does not supersede Shauntae, but I don't fight her either.

There are some things that I do because I am married to the pastor and because I think they're important. When time permits, I enjoy celebrating graduations, retirements, weddings, and the like with congregants. I've seen how much my presence can make a parishioner feel loved and special when I take the time to attend the visitation of their family member who is not a member of our church. I realize that many of these invitations are only offered because I am the pastor's wife. I am comfortable with that. On the flip side, it is important not to allow church members to mold me into their image with all their expectations of who and what I should do or be.

Traditionally, in the Baptist church, the pastor's wife gives leadership to the missionaries. At our first church, the missionaries were 70- and 80-year-old women. I loved that group of women. They had a lot of wisdom, and I marveled at how sharp they were on Sunday morning. I loved sitting with them. But, at 27, I was not going to hang out with them.

I've had people suggest I should sit and serve with the deaconess. I've participated in the dance ministry. At our current church, a woman who knew I had been practicing with the dance ministry before I had ever danced, said, "I want you to think and pray really long and hard about joining this ministry because I don't think Watts is ready for our first lady to dance." I kindly replied, "Thank you. And, I do not allow church members' expectations to determine what I do or don't do." Having self-definition, as opposed to what others impose, is the only way to remain sane in this role.

One of my most interesting experiences has been the journey of wearing my hair natural and being married to a pastor. When I decided to wear my hair natural in 1995, I asked myself the same questions that many women do who have worn relaxers and have decided to go natural. One of those questions is: Would I be able to find a job? To my knowledge, my hair has never been an issue to being in academia. But my hair has had more of an impact on my husband and his profession than my own.

The pastor can often become a central figure to the identity of a congregation. Part of the pastoral package is his wife and his children. Ideally, and for many churches, those images are based on Scripture and Christ-like character. Realistically, tradition, cultural expectations, and the physical image are also considered.

One of the things I dislike most about being a pastor's wife is the Baptist method of "calling" a pastor. The local church "calls" or selects the pastor, usually after an interview process. There are several steps to the process, including what I call the "dog and pony" show. Not only is the candidate interviewed, but the church also wants to see his wife and children. Twice, I was officially interviewed; on other occasions, I was informally interviewed through dinner conversation. Once I was just required to be present at my husband's interview.

Throughout that qualifying process, I learned a lot about black church culture. A pastor's wife's personality and appearance are often factored into their final decision on a candidate. Despite my husband's excellent capabilities, his educational credentials, how well he preached, or what type of "fit" he would have with a church, my hairstyle was mentioned. There are three instances in particular that stand out.

The first instance was at a church in Kansas City, Kansas. It was close enough to my hometown of Kansas City, Missouri, where my family not only attended the Sunday worship service during the candidate process, but knew members in the congregation. My aunt learned from one of her acquaintances why my husband was not selected as the new pastor. According to her friend, "We really liked your nephew. He really could preach, but we could not get with your niece's hair."

Another church, before making their decision, sent a representative to visit the churches of the final two candidates. Over the course of several months, we were visited twice in Cincinnati. On the second visit, the gentleman casually made the comment, "Oh, Sis. So and so was right. Those really are locs in your hair. I thought it was braided on the first visit." I always wanted to say, "And so what was that conversation about?"

At our current church, one of the members on the search committee said, "You know, we thought we were going to hear comments about your hair, but to my knowledge that never came up." I won't say for sure that my hair has hindered my husband's job opportunities, but for sure, my hair has been a topic of discussion among the selection committees.

Though the embrace of natural hair has expanded over the last 20 years, my natural hair violates an ideal image of the first lady in the black church. I was natural when I got married. About three years into our marriage and my husband's first pastorate, I decided to loc my hair. I asked my husband if he had an issue with my hair. His response was, "It's your hair. You can do with it what you want." When we talked about how my hair might impact his job prospects, he said, "I wouldn't go to a church that had an issue with your hair."

I was active in my home church. I had worked in the youth ministry, was a member of the young adult ministry, sang in the young adult choir, taught vacation Bible school, created an annual relationship seminar, and started the women's Sunday school class. Being engaged in the life of the church was not new to me. So, when my husband asked me to wait before I joined a ministry, I was put off. Why should I wait? That didn't make sense to me. He said, "It's more damaging for you to join something and quit later because you didn't like it, or the people, than to wait, pay attention to the people, learn the culture of the church, and then figure out where you belong."

I was even more offended when he told me I was not his choice to give leadership to the women's ministry. To me, I was an obvious choice; not because I was the pastor's wife, but because my spiritual gifts are teaching and leadership. I have a heart for women. Why would you not select me? Eventually, he did give me charge to start and lead that ministry.

For several years, I worked tirelessly in women's ministry until I burned out, which happened right around the time I had our first child. I began to pull back my involvement not only in that ministry, but to some degree, in the church.

Though my husband never verbalized it, I think he liked me being less involved. This was my first insight into understanding what he needed as a wife. The less I was involved, the less commentary I had about the church—what should and shouldn't happen, who said what, what he should do, etc. And that was exactly what he needed: to be able to talk about something other than the church, his job, and the congregants. From the beginning, my husband had given me permission and the freedom to be me. I had to figure out how to do the same for him.

I've watched my husband evolve from a young pastor on fire for the Lord, ready to change lives and change the world, to one who wrestles with cynicism about the church as an institution and the members who are the body of Christ. Any pastor who has been pastoring for any length of time will tell you that his or her job can be likened to leading the Israelites out of the wilderness. They often feel like Moses, who was angry that God sent him to lead "stiff-necked" people, or Jeremiah, who told God, "You tricked me! You sent me to preach to people who would not listen and you knew that!" Pastoring can be a frustrating, lonely, and laborious journey.

My husband has a pastor's heart. He genuinely cares for his congregation and for people. He also is a gifted preacher. Those two things allowed him to go through the motions. He could preach a good sermon, be pastoral by visiting you in the hospital, counsel you, and go to see your son in jail. But the church members could not see he was dying a slow death. He was like a spouse who physically remained in a marriage but had emotionally checked out. It was clear he was depressed, and his drug of choice to self-medicate was food.

He was frustrated that I could not see what he saw. It frustrated me that he didn't see what I saw. Yes, the overwhelming majority of the church was stagnate, complacent, and spiritually lazy, but there was a core—small though it was—who got the vision and wanted to grow. I felt that those were the people he had to focus on, and the rest would come or not.

I felt helpless. I thought my job was to encourage him, be his cheerleader. During that wilderness experience in his ministry, my role became clear. I gained understanding of what it meant to be a wife more so than a pastor's wife. He needed me to provide a solid home base for him and our daughters; he needed a physical and mental outlet away from the church.

Harry is an excellent father who has protected our family time even before we had children. Now, he makes sure he is home between 3:00 p.m. and 6:00 p.m., the time when the girls get out of school, when homework is done, and when he can have dinner with his family before he has to go back to church for various meetings. I carry the majority of the parental load on the weekend because that is his busiest time, filled with Saturday meetings, sermon preparation, and worship. Any deviation has to be negotiated well in advance.

Harry wants me to use my spiritual gifts to serve the Lord in ministry. He's also encouraged and provided a space for me to fulfill my vocational goals and outside interests. In doing these things, I am engaged in ministry only part-time—and he likes it that way. It allows him the opportunity to come home and not have to talk about church or any aspects of his day at the "office." He comes home to a house that is a sanctuary filled with order and love.

I now realize that the best encouragement I can give him is to pray for him. I don't have to speak. Even when he is venting or ranting, I realize he doesn't want or need me to solve the problem; he needs me to be there for him as he lets off steam so that he can continue to interact with the congregation without people thinking he has lost his mind, which they would definitely believe if they got the earful I get! Harry and I have evolved together. I had to learn how to be the help-meet he needed and not the one I thought he needed or the one the church expects me to be.

CHAPTER 3

LOUISE GARR

Married to Rev. Joseph R. Garr
Retired Pastor, Macedonia Missionary Baptist Church
Covington, KY
Interview Date: July 15, 2004

**"And then after awhile, more and more of me came out
and less and less of the 'pastor's wife.'"**

*At the time of the interview, Louise's husband had been retired as a pastor for
eight years. She provides reflection on how she navigated the role of pastor's wife
for 30 years. For her, the role became easier as she defined for herself what it
meant to be Louise.*

M y husband pastored for 30 years. We were married 20 years
before he started pastoring. Nobody told me what my role
was going to be; my husband just said, "Well, just be who you are."
Basically, that's how I got through it; I always called back on those
words he told me.

I was always active; I didn't want to just sit. I did everything
because I liked doing it. I've driven the bus. I've been on the
transportation committee. I've done Sunday school teaching. I've
done vacation Bible school, Sunday school picnics, and director
of Sunday school. I liked being busy, and I liked the children most
of all. Even after I had my youngest baby, I would get up, get her
ready, then drive over to Covington [Kentucky, from Cincinnati]
and take the bus out and pick people up, you know, with my baby!
That was crazy! There were only a few people that would even
consider doing stuff like that, and since I had the strength, and I
could do it, and I just did it.

29

[The congregation] would also volunteer me for a lot of stuff, "Well, Sister Garr can do that, or Mrs. Garr can do that. She likes the kids; she's good with the kids." When we had church election day every year, they'd always put my name up for something that had to do with the children. And sometimes I didn't want to do it. I felt like somebody else should have the chance. I wanted to give somebody else a chance if they wanted to step in and do something. But I liked what I did.

Sometimes I'd get upset because they all think the pastor is God. "Pastor Garr this" and "Pastor Garr that." One day, I just kind of blew up. I said, "You guys always give him his praises and do this and do that." And I said, "What am I, chopped liver!?" They looked at me in a different light after that. I upset my husband about that. He said, "You shouldn't have done that." I said, "Why not? Because that's the way I was feeling. I didn't want to have a stroke because I was keeping this stuff all bottled up inside of me." I know he's the pastor, and I'm his wife, but I just felt like they were overlooking me. It wasn't spite or being mean. They just didn't know any different.

When they were going to give him an anniversary, they wanted to just honor him. It would just be Reverend Garr's anniversary. It was never ours together. I didn't say anything for a long time. And then one day, I talked to him about it, and I said, "I don't think you know how I feel because when they make all these preparations and the things that they want to do for you for your appreciation day, I feel like I'm an afterthought." I said, "I really don't think that's fair because I am your wife. I have a lot of feelings that I don't know quite what to do with, and I don't want to let them explode in the wrong way." I was feeling like a quiet rage there for a while.

He said, "No, honey. It's not that. You have to remember these people are from the older school and they always put the pastor up on the pedestal. Of course, they want you to share in whatever they do for me."

I said, "Well, then why don't they acknowledge it?" The next year, it was Reverend and Mrs. Garr's Anniversary or Appreciation Day. He must have told somebody that because it was resolved. I don't know why I felt that was important, but to me it was. Just that simple fact that he has a wife and a family, and it's not just all about him. Sure, he's the pastor, and I give him his due. He did a lot. But that's no reason for you to exclude his wife.

The first seven or eight years were the hardest. The most challenging thing to me was how was I going to be the person that I really was; how I was going to keep myself there and then be the kind of person that I was supposed to be as the pastor's wife. I had no clue and how to get these two people to come together and be as one and not be unhappy about it. I just felt like if I didn't do the things that I was supposed to do or the way they thought I was supposed to do them, then that would be a put down on him, and I didn't want them to ever say anything about him because of me.

Sometimes you don't feel like talking or being involved and staying to yourself. You had to go to the meetings, and you had to go to rehearsals, and sometimes I just didn't want to do that. So, I played who I was for them and who I really was for me. Then after the talks that we had, it got easier and easier for me. After a while, more and more of me came out and less and less of the "pastor's wife." She disappeared, so I had to be me a lot again toward the end.

My husband told me, "You can't hang out with the parishioners. They cannot be your bosom buddies." So, I didn't have that type of a friend in church. After I had Courtney [my youngest daughter], there was one other little girl that was her age, and they became friends. Her mother and I became friends, and she was about the closest friend that I had. I could really unwind and be who I was.

Sometimes she would invite me and the kids to come over after church if we were going to stay [for an afternoon service] that day. I'd go over to her house, and we'd have Sunday dinner together and then watch TV and listen to the news—all kinds of stuff. We just had a good time. And she was about the closest friend that I had during all the whole time. I don't know why she was so different. I cannot put my finger on it. She passed away not too long ago, and I really miss her. She was just so down to earth; she wasn't doing it for any ulterior motive. And I knew she loved me.

There were four or five women that had eyes for my husband, but he kept me informed, and I trusted him, so I didn't really worry about that. One time we were going on a trip. This one woman in particular was probably about 20 years younger than I am. They didn't know that I was going to go on the trip, and I didn't get there until late. It was something that she did to make me know that she was flirting because women know when other women flirt. We're not stupid.

Honey, I don't know what I said, but I just marched up on the bus, and I just looked her right in the eye, and I said something like, "It's not gonna happen." And she got up out of the seat, and I just sat down beside him. I just kind of said it under my breath. She knew what I was talking about because she got up and left. My husband did not have a clue. He said, "Oh, you made it." I said, "Yeah, I made it." I was so cool. I said to myself, "Oh, yes. I did that good!"

I think the most rewarding thing is the lives that I have touched and how someone else knowing me has made a difference in their life. I must have done something right because one young man just called me the other day. I hadn't heard from him or talked to him in maybe four or five years. But he always will call and leave a message, and that was very rewarding.

I got a card from a lady that I had known for a long time. It wasn't just a role that I was playing; I really meant something to them. I made their life better by the person that I was. I know it's made me a better person.

I don't think a pastor is any better than his wife. I really don't because we do a lot of stuff behind the scenes that no one will ever know about.

CHAPTER 4

ANDREA HAYLES
Married to Bishop Gary Hales
Tabernacle Baptist Church
Lincoln Heights, OH
Interview Date: October 19, 2004

"God told me, 'You need to start protecting your children.'"

When Andrea's husband was called to pastor his first church, their daughters were ages eight and three. Children who are thrust into the first family role often have to adjust more than children who were born into it. Andrea shares how she and her oldest daughter, Kristina, have navigated the role as pastor's daughter while dealing with the normal experiences of coming-of-age that many girls have.

There is a golden rule in our house: Whatever goes on in our house stays in our house. There was a situation when we were going out of town one weekend, and one of the ladies in our church happened to ask my older daughter, "Well, what are you all doing this weekend?" I wondered to myself, "Why would an adult ask a child what are you doing this weekend?" I would expect a question like that from a child but not from a grown woman.

That weekend, we were planning on going out of town, and I think that was the weekend my husband had scheduled someone to preach on Sunday morning, but we didn't want anyone to know. Whenever [the church members] find out that the pastor is not preaching, they don't come to service. So, my daughter just innocently said, "Oh, we are going out of town this weekend; we are going to visit family." Well, it began to circulate. So, the attendance wasn't what it should have been because people found out that the pastor wasn't going to be there. I happened to have seen my daughter talking to the lady, and when we were riding home, I said, "What were you two talking about?"

She said, "Oh well, (I will say her name was Miss Susie) Miss Susie was asking me what we were doing this weekend."

I asked, "What did you say?"

She responded, "I told her we were going out of town this weekend."

I told her, "Honey, you are not supposed to tell what we are doing this weekend. It's no one's business. We have to learn to keep our private lives private." Now, [my husband and I] just don't tell [our children]. We just pop up and do it, so they don't get put in a position where they feel that they are lying or being deceitful.

I realize that it's very hard being a pastor's daughter. There were two little girls that were not speaking to my older daughter. I pulled the girls into a classroom, and I brought the mothers in as well. I said, "Now I understand there are some problems going on because I am watching you all, and you all are not speaking to Christina.. Let me make it real clear. It's hard for Christina because she is the pastor's daughter, and she wants to have friends, and it hurts her when you all don't speak to her. So, what's the problem? Let's work it out."

So, we found out that one little girl was talking about her thinking she's cute and how she doesn't get in trouble because she's the pastor's daughter; she gets preferential treatment. I made it very clear: "No, she's does not. As a matter of fact, you've seen me get on her just like I might confront you all. I am twice as hard on her as I am on you all."

After I talked to the girls and the parents talked to the girls, there was an understanding that they now saw that it's very hard for her. So, we haven't had a lot of issues recently. I am sure there will be something else that will come up. I've prepared my girls to understand at some point and time, you might not have friends in the church. My prayer is that it won't happen, but I want them to be prepared.

God actually told me, "Look, you need to begin to protect your children." My oldest daughter told me that she didn't want to lose any friends because it was hard making friends. And she didn't care how bad they treated her; she wanted to keep them as friends. My response to her was, "Since your self-esteem is not like it should be, I have to protect you. In order for me to protect you, we have to pull in the reigns. You will have to sit with me, sit behind me, or next to me from now on because I don't know what you have to deal with when I am not around you."

She can't really stand and socialize like she used to be able to do. She was devastated that I told her that because she is at an age now where she's at the pre-pubescent stage, not so much a kid anymore. If I am not able to sit with them, then there are three ladies in particular we consider our inner circle. I have told those ladies, if I am not here, the girls need to come sit with you because I don't want them running around, and I need to make sure that they are protected.

I was in constant prayer about the inner circle because the danger is everybody wants to be a part of it. I believe in my heart that God appoints people in your life that are there for a purpose. Those one or two people are part of the inner circle now because their spirits were kind spirits. They struggle everyday like we do to live their life in the manner that Christ wants them to live in. They're encouraging in their words.

I studied a lot of people, and you could always tell who's trying to get in your business and who's just genuine. It will be three years in June [our time at this church], but it probably wasn't until this summer that I acknowledged them as our inner circle because I wanted to take that long to see if they were really genuine, if they were really people that we could trust and could feel comfortable with our children around.

We've acknowledged that our girls need to do some things outside of church. Church is not their life. They're building a relationship with Christ, and we keep giving them the foundation, the keys, but they need some outside interests. My older daughter is learning to play the piano. They want to do some extra sports activities, so we're looking into that. There are things they need to do outside the church and that keeps them balanced.

Our last Wednesday of each month is our Hallelujah Hour service. Well, we don't always go. We stay home. I was at a meeting every Tuesday, Wednesday, and maybe even Thursday. I don't do that anymore. We stay home. We do homework. We do cuddle time. We do those things which are really important.

CHAPTER 5

REVEREND ANN CHAMPION SHAW

Married to the Rev. Robert Shaw
Allen Chapel AME Church
Kansas City, MO
Interview Date: August 4, 2008

"I am who I am, and was when he met me. I'm a preacher first, and then I met a man in ministry."

As a PK (pastor's kid), Ann saw enough in the church that didn't encourage her to want the type of intimacy with the church that most clergy families have. Ann did not imagine accepting her call to ministry as a preacher and marrying a man in the ministry. On her journey, she has learned to negotiate not only her role as a pastor's wife, but to remain true to her ministry calling.

I did not want to preach. I fought my calling. I remember bargaining with God, saying, "Let me be a preacher's wife, but I don't want to preach!" My father, grandfather, and great-grandfather were all preachers, and so I saw a lot of things in the church that weren't good. That was part of the struggle with my call. I didn't want that type of intimacy as a church leader because my heart had been broken even as a young girl. And the joke was on me in the end! I answered my calling in January 1998 and did my trial sermon the fifth Sunday in May 1998.

I met Robert when I was finishing seminary. I was attending Emory Candler, and he was at the ITC [Interdenominational Theological Center] in Atlanta, Georgia. I was at a place of contentment in my voice, identity, and doing what God had called me to do. I hadn't dated in over a year. It was just me and the Lord, and I was loving it. The thought of marriage had not crossed my mind. I was finally at peace with just me and God.

I really do believe, even before our meeting, Robert did have the whole idea of a first lady as a preacher's wife and not necessarily a preacher or minister. I was telling one of the administrators at The Interdenominational Theological Center that Robert and I were engaged, and she then said, "Oh. You know Robert wants a first lady." It was one of those moments where it was just dead silence. I said, "Well, he'll get both." She said, "Okay." It stuck to me because a part of me felt that, too. I am who I am, and was when he met me. I'm a preacher first, and then I met a man in ministry.

The main difference between a preacher and a "first lady" is the ordination. I preach! I'm called. I basically have the credentials to do what any other minister, including my husband, can do. Whereas if I were just a first lady, then I would, of course, not have that access to the pulpit, the preaching, the leading of worship or Communion.

People have always said, "Oh, you're a co-pastor." And I say, "No, I'm an assistant pastor." A co-pastor is someone who's more full-time, more hands-on during the week, and I'm not. If there's something that the pastor wants me to do, I'll take care of those responsibilities. But it's not an equal type of thing. I'm here for the senior pastor.

I'm clear about my call. I know beyond a shadow of a doubt, God has called me to grief and bereavement. I'm a chaplain full-time. There's never been a time when I'm not clear on what I'm supposed to do.

I did a two-year chaplain residency at Research Medical Center and Baptist Memorial Hospital. I offer ministry and prayer support to patients and their families. I deal with a lot of death and the aftermath of that. I've also worked in trauma situations. I did hospice for two and a half years preparing people for the possibility of death. I do spiritual care assessment, seeing where they are and what their end-of-life goals are. The clarity of my call has been a blessing to my marriage because it's helped to create boundaries.

I'm clear: He's the Pastor. I don't have an issue. I'm not trying to be the pastor because this is not what I'm called to do.

We have this thing called tag-team preaching. Rob and I have different styles when it comes to preparing the sermon. People say, "Oh, we love when you guys do the tag-team." You see the product, but it's a fight to get there. We've had our biggest arguments trying to prepare a Word together.

One time, we hadn't been married long, and we were going to do a tag-team sermon at one of the churches, and we had an argument. The devil was riding us. We weren't coming together. I wanted to do one thing. He wanted to go another way. My hair was looking bad; I was having a BHD [bad hair day], and I wanted to wear a hat. He said, "Ann, you can't preach with that hat." I said, "What do you mean I can't preach with a hat?" He said, "You're not wearing it." I said, "I'm wearing my hat!"

Let me just say, the clerical collars came off, and some words were exchanged! I ended up not wearing the hat, but it was a tug-of-war, tension all in the car. We went up in the pulpit mad at each other, and that's not a good thing when you've got to give the Word.

And thank you, Lord, for grace! One of the ministers began to play the song "I Need You to Survive," and something about that song broke that tension, and we walked over to each other and held hands, and we came together and prayed because we knew we could not deliver the Word in that state of mind. God was not going to let us get up and do that knowing there had been great tension between us.

It was really an identity struggle for me having to join my style with Rob's. It felt like I was giving up something. Before marriage, I considered myself established in ministry, preaching as a single woman and used to doing sermons a certain way before joining preaching worlds with my husband through this tag team endeavor. It's cool when you're preaching by yourself, but when you've got to collaborate with somebody else's style and view, that's where that tension comes. Over time, we've worked our way through this. In the end, God blesses, but it's not an easy task.

Speaking of hats, my husband loves hats, and he has asked me, "Ann, are you going wear a hat?" I always tell him I don't have a problem with hats, but I've got to be feeling it. In other words, it's up to me. Most of the time, I don't wear a hat. But when I do want to wear a hat, I go get one!

My mother was the first lady of first ladies. She's just a class act. When she was married to my father and first lady, she had some hats for you. She's still got some of those hats. Some of them she gave away after their divorce, but she was just sharp, head to toe. She was my *en vogue*; she was my essence, so I grew up looking at her, and she fit that mold.

But I noticed that after my parents divorced and she stepped out of that role as first lady, the hats eventually went back in the hat boxes. I've never really had a heart-to-heart talk with her about it, but I just kind of knew that the hats reminded her of her status and where she was. And for her, the hats faded out with her no longer being a first lady.

My father encouraged me when I came into the ministry, and he was my biggest cheerleader. He said, "Just be yourself. Do not lose your femininity." For him, there were some women in ministry who took on masculine tendencies, so he was just encouraging me to keep my femininity: Wear your lipstick. Wear your make-up. Keep your hair up. Wear your nice dresses and suits. They don't all have to be black and dark and toned-down. Just keep your femininity, and let God use the woman in you. I always kept that in mind. Going through the ordination process, we have to wear either black or navy-blue suits. But after that, I said, "I'm going to find me a red suit!"

Now here is something I don't do: When my husband has church board meetings, something an assistant pastor normally would attend because of the role, I don't go. He's the senior pastor, and he's my pastor, too, but he's my husband first. So, if he's presiding over a meeting, and one of the members have something to say that I may disagree with—maybe the tone in which they're saying, the content, etcetera—I'm going to get mad because why? That's my husband first! I'm aware of that so I don't go, and that's one thing Rob and I have never had an issue with. I have to love these people, and I'm reminded of why my Grandma Champion always would say, "You've got to just love in spite of, baby."

I know in order for me to love these people I cannot be at meetings and witness them rudely expressing their grief or whatever. To whatever entitlement they may think they have, there's a way you can express yourself that is respectful. I'm going to hear it anyway because my husband will come home and tell me. But, I don't need to experience it "live and in person" because it takes on a different nuance when you hear it live than when you hear it second-hand.

I take that seriously as far as "loving people even in spite of." We're called to love, and sometimes it's hard to love when you know certain things. But because God lives in me, God gives me the strength to love anyway. You've got to pray your way through that. In my prayer life, I ask the Lord to "create in me a clean heart," especially when those darts are being thrown. My human feelings are real, so spiritually, I have to work through these struggles in my relationship with God. We're called to love. We're called to be mature. We are called to rise, even above the mess.

My husband was assigned here before we were married. He was assigned here the same night he proposed to me, November 1, 2002. So, he was already here, and I was in Atlanta, so we had that whole transition thing going on. And then I joined him in Kansas City, August 2003, after our honeymoon.

Women can be a trip. I've heard stories of women kind of looking, thinking, saying, "Oh, I wish I was a first lady." But, I'm thinking, "You just don't know!"

It's a challenging role when you think about it. My heart really goes out to Robert. I know when he's having a challenging time at church and dealing with things and trying to get people to see the vision. There are even times when the enemy seems to come at him on every end. My heart goes out not only to him but to all pastors.

I mean, being a PK, I would see my dad come home from a meeting, go in the freezer, get a half a gallon of ice cream, and just stand at the counter and just eat. I knew his mind was on issues at the church. But now, being on this side and seeing my husband, my heart goes out to him. He has a tough job. If people really knew what pastors, especially black pastors, go through. I just wish they could just be a pastor for a week so they could really know the struggle.

For the pastors' wives, we have to be our husbands' support. It's not about being some kind of celebrity, though people place you on a high pedestal. Lots of people look up to you. That's the real challenge because we're human, too. We're not perfect people and we have our issues. Yet it is a wonderful thing to be able to do God's work and to minister to God's people.

CHAPTER 6

GAIL DUDLEY

Married to Rev. Dr. Kevin Dudley
The Church at North Pointe
Columbus OH
Interview Date: August 1, 2006

"*I will never get close to church people again.*"

Finding friendship within in the church seems like a natural place to do so as a lay person. However, for a pastor and a pastor's wife, it can be complicated. Gail shares a painful experience and one of the dangers pastors' wives may face when developing friendships with members of their church. When her husband was called to pastor his first church, Gail developed a friendship with a woman that turned sour. As a vibrant, outgoing, people-person, she faced a difficult bind of having to establish boundaries when that was contrary to who she is.

I was too familiar with people because it is in my nature to do so. I am an outgoing, friendly person. I love people. I enjoy being around people. But, in the long run, I realized there are some people you choose to be friends with who may end up being relationships that are inauthentic.

There was one woman, in particular, that I became very close to, even down to exchanging birthday gifts, exchanging Christmas gifts, attending special events, sharing personal conversations, and taking trips. At a certain point, I began purchasing expensive gifts because I had felt our relationship grew to that level. Up until this point in my life, I never really bought nice gifts for anybody but my family. The moment I let my guard down, this person whom I had grown to love as a friend and a sister turned on me. I would hear troubling conversations surrounding this woman and took it upon

43

myself one day to ask questions. I soon learned she was the main spirit spewing many rumors and directly lying on me and to me.

I befriended this woman at a time when I was seeking new relationships after moving to a new city away from family and friends. She was the one person who introduced me to the city, people, and the church membership. Kevin [my husband] was tied up in getting established in the community and building the church. The kids were in school doing what they were doing. All of my friends were elsewhere. I just wanted somebody to talk to, somebody to kick it with. And, honestly, she opened up her arms.

She was the first one to approach me: "Hey, how you doing?" She was the one who (which I know now was not right) would say, "Watch out for this person." I'm thinking, okay, she's protecting me. She was pretty much the person who knew the land of the church and the person other women of the church sought out for guidance, although she wasn't married to anybody in a pastor's role. Everyone loved her. She would do anything for anybody, a really loving spirit—I thought.

I was open and vulnerable sharing all kinds of things; she would share, too. We would discuss church and city business from her perspective due to her husband being a significant public figure in the community and within the church. She gave me that feeling of comfort that allowed me to open up and share encounters I had with others around the church. Some encounters would be good and others not so good.

I truly allowed my guard to come all the way down because I thought I could talk with her in confidence. I was excited to have a friend in the area and someone I could speak with pertaining to the church.

Things began to change, especially the last year and a half, two years for us. For instance, I would receive invitations to events that she used to be invited to attend. I will never forget when she made the comment, "Well, I used to get invited to this stuff until you moved to town. Now I don't get invited." Now she was laughing, but I felt through her laughter she was sharing how she truly felt. I started to see changes.

People began making comments from older and younger women, "Okay, she's competing against you." High school girls could figure that out in a minute. People were seeing it, but I actually defended her for the longest. But one day, the Lord told me I needed to back away. As soon as I backed away, it's like she just upped the ante. She wasn't getting information any more, and when you're no longer in that space, what do you do?

Mrs. Bernice Troy [former first lady of Second Baptist Church in Columbus, Ohio], whom I consider to be a wise woman, taught me that church members weren't my friends. She told me that going in. She taught me to be very prayerful. She told me to be a woman of wisdom, to be wise. She told me to be cordial, but not to make friends. She said those women are not your friends. She told me that. I was just thinking, "Yeah, yeah, right." You know, this is a new generation. I'm thinking she was coming from the old school. When I look back over the five years at our first pastorate, that woman never lied! I will never get close to the people in the church, again. I'll be nice, be cordial, but not attach myself to anybody. I'd rather have friends outside the church.

CHAPTER 7

CANISE Y. BEAN
Married to the Rev. Dr. Michael R. Bean, Sr.
St. Paul AME Church
Columbus, OH
Interview Date: March 9, 2004

"My husband respects the fact that I work outside of the home, and he likes that."

When Canise started to date her future husband, Michael, she was finishing dental school. In addition to desiring to build her career, she had reservations of what the role of a pastor's wife would entail. As with many women, pastors' wives are no different. They make career sacrifices for the sake of the family and marriage. In the African Methodist Episcopal Church, pastors are appointed to a church annually, which could present a challenge to maintaining a dental practice. Canise learned to trust God, support her husband, and be herself.

I met my husband while I was in dental school. He was pastoring part-time, and he was finishing up his master's in Christian education in Dayton, but he would go to Belpre, Ohio on the weekends to his church. I was thinking I really want to move beyond what this man does and to see him for who he is. If I am honest, I was hesitant about marrying a pastor or a preacher. I had this vision that you had to really walk the straight-and-narrow. You had to be a model and pretty much be perfect. I knew that I would fall short of that mark.

We had detailed conversations about how he saw his spouse and her role in the ministry. After talking with him in great detail, I came to realize that he really wanted me to be happy in whatever I did and work in the areas in which I felt I had the most to offer and felt most comfortable. It was not necessarily following the traditional roles. I thought this guy is just too much of a gem to let go. I didn't want to look back and say I'm sorry I didn't at least give it an opportunity.

My number one role is to support my husband and be there for him. Even though he's doing what he loves doing, it is a very giving profession. It takes a lot out of him, and he fails to realize that. Sometimes it's just a simple touch or a simple look or to leave him in peace to have some quiet time. What does he expect of me? I think to just love him. To be completely open and honest with him when I don't necessarily agree with how he handles something. If he does something good, I should tell him that, too.

Second, my role is to be myself. I do not think that the minister's wife has to wear a hat every Sunday or has to outwardly display her faith or has to quote Scripture every time you greet her. Yet, in being herself, she should also be a model so that you really can tell that the minister's wife is not just talking the talk, but also walking the walk.

As a couple, we have been appointed to two churches. Our first church was Quinn Chapel AME Church in Cleveland, Ohio. After ten years, we were moved here to St. Paul AME Columbus. The first move was not an easy one for me. At that time, I was in private practice with three other dentists. I just really felt like I was getting a handle on running my own business. I hated to think about the blood, sweat, and tears that I put into growing my practice and then after ten years looking to sell it and move on.

My son was in first grade, and I wanted him to finish first grade in Cleveland where we had already gotten established. I had settled in and met some wonderful friends, and I was enjoying the culture that Cleveland had to offer. Therefore, we made an agreement that we would certainly let Michael finish his first grade year in Cleveland, and we commuted on the weekends.

At first, I thought, well, it's just a couple of hours, so we can do this on a regular basis, right? After we had commuted for a couple of months, I said, "No, I can't do this." I'm going to have to move. And I wasn't real sure that I wanted to go through the same thing again, the sacrifices in trying to set up my own practice yet again. So, I thought I'm just going to kind of relax a little bit and save money and try to see what we're going to do with our new home, the parsonage. So, what would I do if we were to move again? I would probably think long and hard and not be very ecstatic about it, but I have to keep in mind that it is the reality of the AME Church; it could happen. I do not dwell on it.

I have been blessed to be very well educated. My profession offers a lot of variety that I could pursue if we were to move. Therefore, I would accept that's what God has in His plan for me. So, I don't think of it really as living year to year to year, but then that's somewhat how it is. There is just too much that I want to accomplish and do for others. I cannot be dwelling on if I am going to be in a specific location next year.

My husband respects the fact that I work outside of the home, and he likes that. He wants me to have my independence. At both churches, my husband, if not the first Sunday, the very next Sunday, would let the people know, "This is my wife, and my wife has her own career, and she will determine where her fit is here in the congregation. So, give her a little space, a little time, and it will all work out fine." He always kind of paved the way for me.

Early on in our ministry at our first church, we had a member who had three daughters. One daughter was the same age as mine, and so we became friends. We started doing things together outside of the church. As the relationship progressed, I realized that we had different definitions of *friend*. I felt that she was somewhat using me and not being the true friend that I was attempting to be to her. I pretty much severed the relationship because I just didn't think that I could trust her. There were some things I would think I was telling her in confidence, but then later on I would hear it from another source.

Looking back, I probably could have handled my refusal to enjoy her company outside of the church a lot better. Nevertheless, this experience did help me with future relationships and helped me to understand that being friends with congregants was not my role. I came to realize that my role is not to be a buddy or a good friend with all the members. I can, to a certain degree, be a model for them, but I do not think I can be a friend to all of them.

One of the biggest challenges for me has been the one or two members who have made their main mission in life to see my husband fail or to do whatever they can do to bring him down. They are thorns in my side. It is difficult for me to look these people in the eye or greet them or converse with them without really giving them a piece of my mind. I am aware that that would not necessarily make the situation better.

I have also found that these individuals do not necessarily come across that way with me. They come across in a way that can be interpreted as "Oh everything's wonderful, you're just so great, and I'm concerned about your wellbeing." But they really are slithery like snakes. The devil begins to work, and I feel as if I do not even want to talk to them. How dare you come up to me? Don't you think I know how you act with and seek to undermine and demean my husband, the love of my life? Don't you think I know? Therefore, that is a challenge to remain prayerful. There are some people that kind of thrive on controversy and mean-spiritedness, and that's not me.

For this role, you certainly have to be strong. You have to be yourself and be certain to have a support system whether that be a good friend, an old friend, a family member, or your mother. Your support could come from another pastor's wife, but you need that support system to sustain you.

CHAPTER 8

DENISE JOHNSON STOVALL
Married to the Rev. L. Charles Stovall
Munger Place United Methodist Church
Dallas, Texas
Interview Date: August 1, 2008

"I realized as a pastor's wife, I was called to write about mission."

In many clergy families, especially when the husband is the pastoral leader, his job often dictates where the family will live. However, in journalist Denise Stovall's case, the tables were turned. When her husband was serving as pastor at a United Methodist church in Atlanta, the international newspaper, the United Methodist Reporter, recruited her and her husband to Dallas. It was through her husband's commitment to mission work in Africa that Denise discovered her calling was to write about mission, and that has shaped her career.

Stovall and I met when I was pledging Delta Sigma Theta Sorority, Sigma Chapter at Clark College (now Clark Atlanta University) in Atlanta. He went to the girl who was over with the pledgees and said, "I need somebody to help me with my English class." Everybody knew I was the wordsmith. I was on the school newspaper. I even was working at a television station.

So, I'm coming to the dorm with a pen and paper, thinking I'm going to be helping him with work, but he started telling me about him being in a band and in a fraternity, Phi Beta Sigma. He played keyboard in a band. It wasn't as raunchy as it is now in this millennium, but it was what they called funk music. He'd play on the weekend; then he'd play for his dad's church on Sunday morning. I was fascinated because I thought, "Now how does your daddy let you play this kind of music?" He would take me to places in Atlanta to hear him play, and then he invited me to go to church with him on Sunday.

When we graduated from college, he felt he should be a different physician (he was a pre-med major). He felt the call to heal people spiritually, so he went to seminary. I thought, "I guess I'll hang with this person and see what happens." I was still Ms. Media Person. I worked at all the media in Atlanta. I was a writer for all the black presses, and I mean I worked. I got tired of doing that, and I was offered a job doing public information for Clark College.

Stovall was ordained in 1979 and became a missionary for The United Methodist Church in Zambia. He was in Africa writing me these letters, "We're going to get married." I'd get the letters and say, "That's nice, but I'm still Ms. Journalism." I interviewed a lot of famous people—The Isley Brothers, Aretha Franklin—that's where my head was.

He was in mission with The United Methodist Church, and he came back from Africa and said, "I want to have them do things in Africa." I said, "That sounds good. I will help you." Bu, I just didn't imagine that I'd be really doing that. We got married in 1981, and he was at a church in Atlanta, and he started talking about all he wanted me to do. They'd have these women's meetings in mission at 11 o'clock. I said, "No way, Jose, because the news comes on at noon." I had to make sure I was at the station for the noon news. I got them finally to change the meeting to the weekend.

I'm doing my media work; I'm doing the church work and my sorority work. I was the PR person for the whole chapter in Atlanta. I was the public relations person for *Ebony* Fashion Fair [co-sponsored with the sorority]. I'm juggling like in a circus. I had to ask, "What's priority?"

The thing that made me come full circle and realize my calling was to help him with his mission work was I would hear the stories

52

the people from Africa would write him. They would come to Atlanta. He'd open our house, and I'd say, "We are having these strange people stay on the floors." But, he would say to them, "Whatever you want, take, do." I'm thinking, "Is this how it's going to be?"

It was hard at first getting used to, but I really just began to enjoy it when I met the women. The women were so appreciative of somebody helping them with simple things like telling them how they can take care of their children and helping them with education. They were so grateful to just get books, and they enjoyed my writing. I didn't have to beg them to read my writing. So, I decided I'm going to do what I can to help these ladies in Africa. So, I became Ms. Mission Lady.

I have to say, some of the stories I wrote about Africa were powerful in Atlanta. There were some people in Atlanta for a conference, and I gave them a tour of Clark. One of the gentlemen said, "I like what you wrote. Are you interested in a job?" I said, "I don't know. This is a good job here." He gave me his card. His name was John Loveless. He was from Dallas, and I thought, well, I can't go because my husband has a church here.

He called me again a couple of months later. I told Stovall, "They like my writing. They want me to come to Dallas." He said, "Dallas? You don't know anything about Dallas except the television show." I said, "Yeah, but they love my writing. Somebody loves my writing! I want to go!"

It was almost a year, and, finally, I think his dad really convinced him. His dad said, "Well, she's a good writer, and the people like her writing, and they need a black woman." The publication had a person of color, one woman, but she was getting ready to leave to go into the ministry. They just called and called and called, and they said, "Just come to Texas and see if you like it." They paid for me, Stovall, and our son, Leonard, who was three years old at the time.

I told them, "I will come if you find my husband a church. Now you have to find him a decent church. He's got to get a good appointment." I said, "And if I come, I promise you, you will not regret it. People will know that you are serious about mission." I went in February 1987, little Leonard and me. Stovall stayed in Atlanta until June.

I appreciate him doing that because he's from Atlanta--his mother and father, all his relatives were there. He was one of the co-founders of The Concerned Black Clergy in Atlanta that's known all over the state of Georgia, but he left and came here because I wanted to write.

I felt because he did that for me I needed to do something that could show him I appreciated him and something that could help him do what he wanted to do.

I was doing a story in New York, and they were electing people to be delegates with the World Council of Churches to be monitors for the first all-African election in South Africa. I said, "I know somebody perfect," and I put his name in the hopper. I called people; I called my friends. I said, "You all get my husband elected." He got elected, and he was one of only two people representing The United Methodist Church in the United States.

But I got sick. I was in the hospital, and I didn't know what was wrong. They found out I have MS. I said, "Why couldn't this happen five years ago? Why couldn't this happen in the future? Why does this have to happen in 1994, Lord? Why, why, why, Lord?" Stovall said, "No, I can't go. I need to stay here with you." I said, "Honey, I called my friends. I wrote letters. I begged. You're going to South Africa. This is history." So, we flew my mother to Dallas to stay with me.

Stovall was there at Nelson Mandela's inauguration. When he and Winnie came to the United States, he hosted Winnie. A lot of people said, "Oh I wouldn't have let my husband go." I said, "Honey, you don't know me." I told him, "You better get on that plane," and I don't regret it.

He was there all summer. At first, he wrote letters just to me. But then when I read the letters, I said people will want to read about this. I published them and called it "From South Africa, With Love." I sent it to the papers in Dallas, and they printed some of them. They even talked about it on the ABC affiliate here. Every time he would send me a letter, I printed it. I made hundreds of copies, and I mailed it to every church member, and they would read it every Sunday morning at church.

I'll never forget that they had a picture of him as he carried a woman to the poll. She was in her nineties and could not walk. It was the first time she was ever allowed to vote in her life! She did not know how to spell her name; all she did was put an X in that box.

Everybody knew I loved writing about Africa, so when I got better, I was flown to Africa. Stovall and I have been to countries all over Africa. We went to help people in the villages. I would work with the ladies. He'd teach Bible studies to the men. I've been to Burundi, Rwanda, Kenya, Zambia, Zimbabwe, the former Zaire (it's now called the Democratic Republic of Congo), South Africa, and Mozambique. He and I went to Kenya together. I realized as a pastor's wife, I was called to write about mission.

On the other hand, I am not the traditional first lady. I missed Women's Day one year, and some of the women were angry with me. They sent me a picture of all these ladies in red, and a lady said, "We had on our red, but you are not in the picture. You know you should have been there, but you were over in Africa." I said, "True enough, but the people in Africa appreciated me being there, and I know I was serving God doing it. I'm not being ugly, but I could wear a red dress anytime."

Some of the people I helped have gone to glory because of the war in Rwanda. But those ladies in Africa appreciated me helping them, so I would rather do that.

My MS really has gotten worse. It's just really hard for me to rest, even when I get tired. It hurts. Sometimes I cry. I have offers to write things I wish I could do, but I can't. If I've got to write a story, I'll crawl to the computer table and write. If it's something that's happening—and I guess its vanity—I want to be the first one to do it. I want to have the scoop. That's one thing about me. If I want to write, I'm going to write.

I know a lot of the clergy people, and very few have had my experience. A lot of people have to move, but the tables were turned because I got offered the job. I was the first black associate editor of this international paper. Then I became director of corporate communications. They flew me all over the world. I'd be in the airport writing my story on the computer. I would print it, fax it, and then switch planes. I'd go to Kennedy to fly back to Dallas, and it'd already be in the paper. I've loved it, but it wore me out.

I really appreciate my husband moving for me. People think he was born in Texas. I don't say it a lot, but when they talk about, "Oh you know, Mrs. Stovall, you need to be proud of your husband because he's perfect for Texas." I just smile and nod because they don't realize he came to Texas because of me.

Mrs. Denise Stovall passed away on January 19, 2016.

CHAPTER 9

DIANNE CLEAVER
Married to the Honorable Rev. Emanuel Cleaver, II (D–MO)
St. James United Methodist Church
Kansas City, MO
Interview Date: March 2004

*"I've never felt like just Emanuel Cleaver's wife. Of
course, it depends on what circle I'm moving in. In civic
contexts, Emanuel Cleaver's wife is more significant
than other arenas. But that has never impacted how I felt
about myself."*

*Culturally, in the African American church, pastors and their wives are often
esteemed and set apart. While she acknowledges there are some benefits to the
role, Dianne has enjoyed the experience of being treated like a regular member.
However, by being married to the first African American mayor of Kansas City
and current US Congressman, Dianne has experienced the perks and trials of
being a politician's wife. She juggled both roles, as well as those of wife, mother,
community activist, and career woman while continuing to define what all
meant to and for her.*

Emanuel answered his call to ministry about three years after
we got married. I didn't know enough to think ahead about
what the role might be; I was raised Catholic. The thing about
our church that is very interesting is Emanuel and I grew up with
our church. When we went to that church, it was a little run-down
building with a leaking ceiling that had 25 members.

As Emanuel built the church, I would say the bulk of the
people were around our age; it was a young church. I had really
never felt any pressure to do or be more. I was always working; I

was always involved in other things. Also, there were a lot of people who wanted roles in the church—men and women who wanted to chair this or head that, so why should I get in competition with them when that's not really where my interest lies.

I am the second-longest standing member of our choir, which is like ever since Emanuel came to the church thirty-one years ago. The women's organization would be the other organization in which I've been most active. In the women's group, I am just a member; I'm not an officer. As far as use of my time, that wasn't something that seemed too appealing, and it seemed like a lot of other people were more interested in taking those roles. I certainly understand in a smaller church everyone needs to do more. I used to go to more things. There was a point when everything the church was having, I would go—every afternoon program, every youth program—I would be in attendance in the earlier days, but not now.

My role is supporting Emanuel in his role and supporting things that the church does. One of the main things I have done to support him is take on the extra responsibilities because of his time, whether it was things with the kids, the house, or personal finances. I have had double duty. That has allowed him to spend the amount of time he needed to spend at the church and other things.

I went to work when my twins were three. Then after they got up in age, compiled with Little League, Girls Scouts, Boys Scouts, I was tired, and their father was gone to a meeting every night. I think another way of being supportive is to be unselfish of demands other people have on your time—the time of day, night or weekends, family issues, deaths, whatever—just to be very accepting and not let it become a point of contention. You accept that as part of your role.

We have four children, and I'm sure my kids were on display, but it just didn't bother me. When the twins were young—six, seven, eight, I don't know—people used to call them Evil Knievel and

58

Awful Knofel. It wasn't serious trouble; they were just rambunctious and into everything. I don't think I would have done anything differently. I might not have gotten up that early to get them there if their daddy hadn't been the pastor. I do think that St. James is a good church family, but how do I think they've been impacted? It's not something they talk about, but [my children] do talk about being a politician's child.

It is really hard to separate Emanuel as a preacher-politician. It all blends together after a while in his career as pastor and politician. So, when people say I am Emanuel Cleaver's wife, what are they saying? Are they saying Emanuel Cleaver the preacher or politician?

I've never felt like just Emanuel Cleaver's wife. First of all, he came to my town. There are just a lot of people I know and who know me from growing up. And my mother was raised here, so I've never felt like just his wife. And, then, I've always had a career. I was a pastor's wife, and then I became mother of the twins: "Are you the one with the twins?" Between my family, my friends, and my career, I have never felt that way. I've always felt like my own person. Sure, people who don't know me ask, "Aren't you Emanuel Cleaver's wife?" Of course, it depends on what circle I'm moving in. In civic contexts, Emanuel Cleaver's wife is more significant than other arenas. But that has never impacted how I felt about myself.

There are certainly more perks to being a politician's wife than a pastor's wife, especially with the egalitarian nature of our church, along with not a lot of expectations of me. One of the benefits of being a pastor's wife is being intimately involved in the life of the church. That doesn't mean the groups and activities, but more the spiritual, feeling like it is your spiritual home and spiritual life as the church evolved and grew.

I don't get a lot of "Oh, here's your parking space," Or "Let me bring you your plate." Maybe when Emanuel comes down [to the fellowship hall] someone might offer to fix him a plate. I don't act like the first lady of the church, so in a lot of ways they treat me like another member. I'm sure in some ways they don't. Everyone knows I'm the pastor's wife maybe because people have seen my picture. When members of our church have relatives in town, they introduce me. Or people say, "This is the first time I've met you, and I've never really seen you before. I go to eight o'clock service." But other than that, I have some place to hang my coat and keep my choir robe.

There are, however, lots of perks to being a politician: the fancy dinners and tickets that you don't pay for. I got to go on some great trips that we traveled for cheap. We went to Japan, and we were the sister city of the World's Fair in Spain, and it was in Seville. There was a baseball pass we traded in to get tickets for most games. We got invited to most Chiefs' games. It was awesome. The thing I miss most when he left the mayor's office is we had a parking pass at the airport.

There are a lot more drags, too. Everyone knows who you are. You're kind of an easy target. Talk about some other people! I'm not that interesting. Then there is the criticism of him. The harshest criticism from critics usually gets back to him before it gets back to me because he spends more time with the church. The things I do hear probably come from the friendlier critics, the ones who are welcome to say it so that you can handle it.

You can either say something or try to give his perspective if you know it, but my husband might not be around, so I'll reply, "Oh, I'll check that out. I'll look into that." Sometimes you're going to get upset, and you tell them, "Did they know this?" or "Did they have this information?" or "That's just not correct," but you're usually talking to an intermediary, not talking to the critic. You can always find something that wasn't correct in the newspaper. That's the downside of political life: The media are in control.

Being a pastor's wife is a calling, but it doesn't mean we don't have other callings. We all have multiple roles: career, personal, mother, volunteer, etc. It's a calling to do well, but it doesn't

60

necessarily mean that it's your only calling.

I think there are some things about my personality that have made it easier for me. Outside criticism doesn't bother me that much. I'm a pretty confident person, and I don't need everyone to love me. You have to remain your own person.

My advice for other pastors' wives would be to choose your role in life. To the extent to which you wanted to be a pastor's wife, make sure that's a personal decision and not something that someone or some organization is pressuring you to do. To the extent that you want to have a role outside of the church, make sure to make time to do that because then you will be more satisfied with what you are called to do.

CHAPTER 10

PAMELA WOODEN

Married to Bishop Patrick L. Wooden, Sr.
Upper Room Church of God in Christ
Raleigh NC
Interview Date: July 24, 2008

"I've been through things as a pastor's wife, as a woman, as a wife, as a mother—things I've had to suffer, just the regular everyday things that were my lot—but I couldn't imagine going through life without Christ and a good husband in my life."

Pamela was young when she married Patrick. He had already accepted his call to preach, which enabled her to accept the role of first lady with ease. While the position has afforded her many things she had never dreamed of, it is her walk with Christ, first and foremost, that has sustained her on the journey, especially during a devastating time with her family.

I have heard stories that some pastors' wives have had with embracing the calling and accepting it, but I was very young and really didn't know anything else. I had only been out of high school for a year when I married, so my feet were not planted in a career or anything like that. It was not a struggle for me. I embraced it wholeheartedly and considered it an honor to have been chosen by Patrick and the Lord, to take this journey through life with him.

We pursued ministry together, which is something that I certainly attribute to us being together 28 years later and still being happily married. We have always gone in the same direction. We have always pursued the same goals. As a matter of fact, I have always pretty much embraced the ventures that the Lord has sent him on. His vision became my vision. I put my career, my education, my ambitions on hold and pushed him and his vision.

I felt that my role was pretty much to support my husband in what he was doing. In the beginning, I did not see it as a calling on my life as well. I saw it as something that the Lord had called him to and that it was my responsibility as his wife to support him, keep the home, and to raise our children.

[My perception of the role] has changed quite a bit in that I do see it as a calling upon my life now. Although I am considered to be a stay-at-home mom and don't work a secular job, I do work extensively within the ministry without receiving a salary. I have accepted the call of the Lord on my life to minister His word, and I assist my husband in ministry in whatever way I can. Therefore, I see ministry as my occupation.

It is not based upon a paycheck, but it is what I love to do and what I believe the Lord has called me to do, not on the same level as my husband, of course. But the Bible tells us to work while it is day, for when the night comes, no man can work. I must add that although I don't receive a salary, my husband and the Lord have rewarded me greatly. I am extremely blessed!

I serve as the vice president of the ministry and president of the Women's Department. Additionally, I oversee the administrative functions of the ministry, which includes serving as president of our school's board. I'm not a co-pastor because it needs to be clearly understood that the church has one head (the pastor) and that everybody else falls under him, including me. With the pastor being clearly defined as the leader of the church and ministry, it provides understanding and clarity to the membership, the employees, and the officers about who is the final authority in the church.

There are people who believe that if you are a Christian, you're not supposed to suffer anything, and most certainly not if you are the pastor or the pastor's family. I believe that stance is an unbiblical heresy. For the Bible tells us that Jesus suffered and to arm ourselves likewise.

A great challenge for me, however, is living in a fish bowl—always being in the spotlight, especially during times of suffering. A lot of times when I go places, I have to constantly be aware that people know me regardless to whether I know them. I live with the understanding that people are watching me and that nothing I do, nothing I experience, nothing I go through, for the most part, is private.

I would love to, like anybody else, be able to deal with my personal issues privately, but because I'm a pastor's wife, because I'm a public figure, a lot of times everything in my life seems to be on display. That's difficult for me. I've learned over the years, and we've taught our children, that living in the fishbowl is par for the course, so be where you're supposed to be, and do what you're supposed to be doing.

Not too long ago, our family dealt with a very traumatic experience (I will not say what it was because it is not my story to tell), but the Lord sustained us and is seeing us through. It has been a one-day-at-a-time situation where we wake up in the morning and the Lord is there. He gives us courage to go on, strength to hold our heads up and face people who may see, may know, and may wonder how we could handle such a situation.

One of the things my husband did was he told the church about it because we certainly didn't want it to be something that they heard in the streets. We also wanted the church to know that we are human and deal with things, too. We have to trust God, which is the same thing we preach to them and encourage them to do. We have to hold our heads up just like they have to hold theirs up. We all need the Lord. We want them to be able to see that we live by the same biblical principles as they do. Furthermore, to have the prayerful support of the saints has certainly been a major encouragement and a major blessing.

I'm a somewhat quiet, introverted person. I am not very talkative, especially before people that I'm unfamiliar with. Some people can just go in a crowd, spark up a conversation, and talk to anybody. That's just not me.

There are quite a few perceptions of me. It depends on who you ask. I've heard people say that I'm stuck up or that I always keep to myself, which I believe to be something people typically say about pastor's wives because they see us dressed up and see us with a hat on and assume we are a certain way. I don't know, but I wonder if that's the way they would be if they were in our shoes.

On the other hand, I've had people say, "You are quite a down-to-earth person. You are approachable. People can talk to you. You have a great sense of humor." More often than not, that is how people view me once they get to know me.

Sometimes people deal with the pastor's wife based on their relationship with their former pastor's wife. I've had a lot of people to say to me, "I never felt like you were supposed to approach a pastor's wife" or "I always deemed the pastor's wife to be the untouchable." That's not my persona at all because I believe in building relationships and connecting with people. I don't think I'm an unfriendly person, but I do keep to myself a lot. I'm sure if you ask, you can find somebody who thinks I am unfriendly. It is human nature for people, at times, to stereotype and formulate their own opinions about people who are in the public.

My greatest passion and area of interest is the women's ministry. We have been able to be quite a blessing to a lot of women, to enlighten women, to empower women to feel good about themselves, feel good about who they have been called to be in the Lord, and to embrace holiness, godliness, Christian principles that teach them how to work and operate during the varied phases of life as a Christian woman.

To see relationships with women develop, to see women learn how to get along with one another has been a very rewarding experience. That's something that I hold dear to my heart. The rewards, as a pastor's wife, are many in that I like to see people blessed. I like to see people flourish. I've had the opportunity to help people, counsel people who were in a very low state of mind. Then to see them evolve into successful, progressive, independent women has been worth every trial I have ever been through.

Being a pastor's wife has afforded me the opportunity to travel extensively to places that I may not have had the opportunity to go to otherwise. I've been able to broaden my horizons, meet a lot of people, experience different cultures, extend my taste palate with different cuisines, and see historic wonders of the world in places where I've traveled across the country. That has been quite a blessing to me. It has also been an experience that I never thought or dreamed as a young person growing up that I would've experienced.

I have a great husband and family, and the Lord has blessed us to live a very comfortable life. Yes, I have nice things, and some people may say, "Well, she's got it all." For me, things are the blessings of the Lord. They are nice to have, they are enjoyable, and I certainly appreciate and I thank God and my husband for them; but I don't consider things (houses, cars, clothes, jewelry, etc.) to be my greatest rewards in life. A lot of times when people hear this, they think it's being said because it's the right thing to say. But, honestly, my greatest, most cherished rewards are salvation; the peace, joy, and security that come with serving the Lord; a loving husband and family; and good friends, to name a few—now, to have this and things is wonderful!

I've been through things in life as a pastor's wife, as a woman, as a wife, as a mother—the things that I've had to suffer, the things that I've had to deal with, just the regular everyday things that were my lot, things that I saw coming, and things that I didn't see coming—but I couldn't imagine going through life without Christ in my life. He has certainly been the difference-maker. Even with being a pastor's wife and with the challenges that are considered germane to us, it is Christ who makes the difference: having the peace and protection of God, the security that all things work together for good to them that love the Lord, the peace in knowing that God is in charge.

It's easy to look within ourselves to try to work it out, figure it out, fix it ourselves, but we grow to the point where we understand that God is in charge and that we have to trust in Him and not lean to our own understanding. Life also teaches that as important as ministry and the church are, they are not as important and should not take the place of marriage and family. It takes a lot of hard work to keep the things of our life in proper perspective.

CHAPTER 11

JOYCELYN LEWIS

Married to Rev. Wendell Lewis, Pastor
Jimtown Baptist Church
Lexington, KY
Interview Date: July 30, 2006

"A woman with a calling is in a lonely place."

Joycelyn's husband has pastored a small country Baptist church outside of Lexington, Kentucky, for a little over two years. She has also been called to preach. While women are affirmed in the preaching ministry in different regions of the country, they are not among the Baptist denomination in Kentucky. This has led to a dilemma as she desires to be both obedient to the Lord and not cause dissension in her home.

Hiding my call is the most challenging thing I've had to deal with. It's still hard to say, out loud, but I've been called to preach. Our church doesn't believe in women preachers—neither the district, the church, nor the people. From what I understand, [church women] go hear one if Juanita Bynum or Joyce Myer came to town. I'm not sure they would receive [the Word] from me. I feel like I have answered my call, but I haven't publicly acknowledged my call in the formal sense of going before the church and saying, "I've been called," and getting licensed.

It started about nine years ago when I felt a calling on my life. I really believe it started when I was young. I've always loved the Word. I can recall coming from church and pretending to re-preach the sermon. My cousin gave me a video tape of a woman who was preaching. I was really touched by the message. I sat in the middle of the bed, watching her, and just cried because it was about dealing with people who mistreat you, which many times had been my experience. I was like, "Man, she is so powerful."

Well, I don't know how long after that I was in a Bible study, and the preacher was teaching out of 1 or 2 Corinthians where it talks about the order of worship referring to the Scripture that said, "A woman should be silent in church." The teacher said, " 'Speak,' translated in the Greek means to preach. And that's why we say women should not preach." Well, it just did not settle well with me. Then I started thinking, "Well, maybe I've done something wrong because I listened to this woman preach." And so now I'm wondering, "Was I in sin for this?"

I had a Hebrew-Greek Study Bible. (I actually looked at it while I was sitting in that class.) I went home and looked in a Hebrew-Greek Study Bible. The word *speak* meant talk, tell. It didn't have anything to do with preaching. I thought, "He lied. Why would he lie?" That was disheartening, in and of itself. I prayed and asked God, "You know, Lord, I'm hearing conflicting things. How about you reveal it to me. Can you tell me the truth regarding the situation?"

I went to a women's conference, and I was mad when I got to the conference and saw all these powerful women preachers. I thought, "They have been keeping this from us."

A woman with a call is in a very lonely place. Who do you talk to? My former church had five women who acknowledged their call and had to leave. They didn't put them out [of the church], they just found some place for them to go, "You know, you can't preach here, but we'll find a place for you to preach." And many times, they were directed to a Methodist church. The hardest part of being a women called to preach in the ministry is there are so few women out there, especially in my area. You don't have somebody that's going to help you with the etiquette of preaching, with the do's and the don'ts. Most men have a mentor, and most women don't. There are more women who are led to the slaughter. They're like sheep out there alone.

When my husband went to interview for this church, I asked him, "Could you please tell them about me?" He never said he would or wouldn't, but he never did it, either. My husband said when he interviewed for the pastorate that they asked him what he believed about women preachers. He said he told them that he believed that women could preach, but they couldn't pastor. Well, I feel like your actions speak louder than your words. He wouldn't allow me to be in a position where I have to hide my calling. My husband says the church is just not ready.

My sister-in-law's pastor agreed to license me from his church. He and my husband talked, they both were in agreement, and they were supposed to make arrangements to have it all done. But when I talked to my husband about it, I felt like he was only doing it just to make me happy, not really because he felt like that's what God wanted him to do.

I said to him, "You know, this is a really big thing, and you can't do it to make me happy. If you just do it for me, then we'll go into this thing weak. You have to do this for God. You have to know that God wants you to do it. There is going to be a time when that's the only thing that's going to keep us, to know that God tells us to do this, tells you to do this especially. And I don't want you to do it just because, 'Oh, I'm just trying to make my wife happy.' He said, "No, that's not why I'm doing it." But it has never happened.

I think he believes he is being supportive. One of the things that he did say was that he was worried about how other men [preachers] will treat me. And he said, "I don't want to have to hurt somebody." I said, "Well, God is the one who is going to handle all that." So, I don't know, maybe he just doesn't have enough faith with regards to my call.

It's not a topic we really talk about. He does not ever say, "No, you can't" if someone invites me to speak somewhere else. I'll come home after preaching somewhere, and it's, "How did everything go? Oh, that's good." That's, pretty much the extent of it. I don't go home and go, "Honey, guess what?" It's not an exciting time between us.

I would love for us to really be in this together. Our church is in the country, most people have a 20-25 minute drive. Well, if you get sick or somehow can't be there, why do you need to call somebody in to bring the Word? I would like him to be a trailblazer. Actually, I believe he's called to be that. I believe that's part of his purpose because God knew he was going to be married to me.

I just think it would at least be easier to answer the call if you are single because you only have to answer the call for God. You know, you don't have this other person. If he [a husband] is not advocating you to do something, then you have to step back. Otherwise, it will cause dissension in your home.

But God gave me revelation. You could use Mary as an example of when the angel came to her and said, "This is what God wants you to do." She didn't say, "Well, hold on, let me go talk to Joseph." She said, "Yes." But even as I looked at that Scripture, I saw where God used both of them to bring the gift. So, I have to wait on Joseph to have his visitation by an angel.

CHAPTER 12

RITA RUSSELL

Married to the Rev. Stephen J. Russell, Jr.
Calvary Baptist Church
Baltimore, MD
Interview Date: July 31, 2008

"I felt I was very far from the ideal pastor's wife. I was still a babe in Christ."

When Rita's husband, Stephen, was called to pastor his first church in Washington, Pennsylvania, she was plagued with uncertainty and insecurity about what the role would mean for her. By learning to trust and lean on God, she adjusted to the new role of first lady, grew in her own personal walk with the Lord, and also grew in her understanding of how to minister to her husband.

I grew up in a church. We went to Sunday school. We sang in the choir at our Presbyterian church in Pittsburgh. But I never really accepted Christ as my Savior. I knew who Christ was. I knew he died on a cross. I knew about Daniel in the lion's den. I knew all the stories but never what it meant to have a relationship. My husband grew up in a Methodist church, and I think it was similar for him. He went to church with his grandmother because that's what he had to do it.

We got married about two years after we graduated from college. He preached his initial sermon almost exactly two years after we got married. I was a little nervous. We were both new Christians. We didn't get saved or baptized until right before our wedding. It was kind of shocking to me because he matured so fast, and I felt like he was leaving me behind.

We joined Mount Ararat in Pittsburgh because we wanted to find somewhere to get married. We said, "We'll just join this church so we can have a wedding here," not knowing what God had planned for us. We actually did get rooted in the Word, going to Bible study and just being faithful. Within less than a year of us doing that, my husband knew he was called to preach.

I was a little leery not knowing if he was sure this was what he was supposed to do because *I* wasn't sure about what he was supposed to do. I didn't know what it was going to bring for me, the whole idea of being a first lady. What kind of expectations were they going to have for me?

[My husband's first church] was an older congregation, so I was really nervous because I'm not a hat-wearer. People that knew me said, "You have to buy a lot of hats now since you're going to be the first lady." But one person who was a blessing to me was my first lady. She said, "Don't allow people's expectations to change you. God called you to be a first lady just like he called your husband, but he didn't call you to change your ways to fit some kind of mold." I always took that to heart.

I felt I was very far from the ideal pastor's wife. I was still a babe in Christ. I was going to Bible study, learning a lot, growing spiritually, but I didn't feel like I was ready to be a first lady. Are they going to expect me to take over the women's ministry, ministering to groups of people that may be more mature than I am in Christ? Am I going embarrass him because I don't know everything? But it's been a blessing because no one really put those expectations on me.

People ask the typical things like, "Oh, do you sing?" You know, they expect the first lady to sing. No, I don't sing. But my husband made it clear, and especially when we came here to Calvary, that "right now my wife's focus is our family and our children. She has a lot to offer, but give her some room, allow her to let you know where she will fit in and not try to place her in a box." And they've been really wonderful about not doing that.

I learned over the years to just know that [Stephen] trusts the Lord and trusts that God will lead him. The greatest reward for me has been the way my faith has grown. Being in this role, you see a lot of everything. I've learned tremendously how to trust God in everything. We've been to the point where we were just flat broke, no money, no way to pay anything and not knowing where it's going to come to learning that my son has diabetes. Just to see God take me through that process when I thought I would've lost my mind.

The difference between then and now is my faith. None of us are really qualified to do anything. It's all about God and all about what he puts in us. I know that I am qualified to do whatever He wants me to do. He'll put me in a situation where a young lady or someone in the church may be dealing with an experience that I've dealt with, or something that I know that I know that I know. Sometimes I'll start talking and not know where I'm going with it, and then He will bring it all together. I just try to be in tune with Him, always looking to Him, not just acting on my own or jumping the gun.

I'm very careful about the things I say and about how I respond to people, especially when they're having problems, because I know, in the position that I'm in, I'm a representation of our Father. I'm very careful and very prayerful about that all the time.

The hardest thing I've watched my husband go through was at our first church. We had a lot of people who were very hurtful toward him. We came from a situation where we were in a good place as an associate minister. We had an awesome pastor; he just let him work and flow in his gifts. We got called to this church where everything he tried to do got shot down.

Most of the people in the leadership had been in leadership for years. He was only 31-years-old, and they looked at him like he was a little boy. They wanted him to come and just do what they told him to do. So, when he wasn't that, then they fought everything he tried to do. Every single thing he tried to do, they fought.

It wasn't the whole church; it was mostly the leadership of the church. I just watch him be so frustrated. It was just a hard situation pretty much the whole time we were there, and he would come home and just be beaten. We felt like outsiders the whole time we were there.

God has really worked with me on my patience and compassion. I used to be very impatient with people, especially when it comes to my husband. He's the pastor, but he's still my husband, so I am very protective of him, his spirit. I've learned sometimes I have to use that in a different way and not use it in an attack mode. I know one of my issues is getting upset if I feel like someone is disrespecting my husband or is out of line. My husband is very good at keeping stuff from me because of that. But I think he's really groomed me to be able to try to see things through other people's eyes and try to understand where they're coming from instead of just jumping on them and saying, "Don't talk about my husband that way!"

I try to guard my husband's heart by just being there for him. If he's upset about something going on at church, and he's not ready to talk about it, I try to be available when he's ready to talk. Sometimes, it's hard to figure out what exactly I'm supposed to do to help. I just wait to see if he needs me to leave him alone. It's also difficult because you want to know what's going on.

My reaction has changed. The first year, we would have gotten into an argument because I wanted to know what's wrong and he was not telling me. I felt he was leaving me out, and I took it personally. Or I thought that he thought I wasn't good enough to talk to, which, of course, was part of my insecurity in thinking that he was so much more spiritually mature than I was. But now I understand that a lot of the time it's him trying to protect me from being upset or trying to leave it there and not bringing it home. I guess we're protecting each other's hearts at the same time. The "aha" moment for me was when I was cleaning the bathroom one day and I found this journal he has kept since he first started pastoring. At the time, he was going through seminary; he was trying to work, and he wasn't making any money. He didn't think he was supporting his family, and he was dealing with the frustrations at church.

He would come home and not be able to just relax. Instead, he'd come home, and I'd badger him and say, "What's going on? You don't talk to me. I'm your wife; you are leaving me out. I'm a part of this, too." I felt really bad I was adding to his pressure and stress. It let me see that when he comes to you, you need to be the safe place, be the calm place, the place he can relax. It was at that point where I made it up in my mind that I was going to be that for him.

The good thing that came out of Washington (Pennsylvania) was that you know there are going to be trials, there are going to be people who don't like the pastor, or don't want the change he's trying to make. But what did they do with Jesus? They crucified Him, so you know they're going to do the same to you. I take it in stride. It used to upset me sometimes, but now I don't allow it to get to me. I just pray.

It all goes back to my faith and just my trusting God and knowing that he has my back. When you know that, it's like you can deal with anything. I could deal with anything that the enemy brings on because I've seen Him deliver us so many times from different things; and, now, when trials come, I'm, like, "Wow, God, what are you going to do with this?" It's exciting to know that something great is going to happen as a result of a trial that you go through. Hopefully, every Christian experiences that. When they go through and come through trials, they come out stronger and can say, "Bring it on!"

CHAPTER 13

SANDRA CROWDER

Married to the Rev. Kenneth W. Crowder
Metropolitan African Methodist Episcopal Zion Church
Norfolk, VA
Interview Date: May 31, 2008

"I hear a lot of people say, 'I like the pastor, but the pastor's wife is too bossy.' So, many times I try to stay in my lane."

Being a pastor's wife requires a delicate dance between being warm and welcoming, establishing a rapport with other members—especially the women of the church—and maintaining boundaries. Sandra has danced this dance well as she has learned to develop healthy working relationships with other women and not be overbearing at the same time.

Being a pastor's wife is a calling of mine; I have a comfort zone with it. I enjoy church ministry. I enjoy working with the seniors, the youth, young adults, and the children. I enjoy watching my husband have success in his ministry. My role is to assist my husband, to make sure that I can do everything possible for me to do to help him complete his task as the pastor. So, my greatest joy is being a part of the ministry, and I don't want to just say a successful ministry because there have been challenges at churches and with the people and with things that he wanted to accomplish. But to be there to watch a situation that wasn't so bad become a better situation is a joy.

They have a joke and they tease me that I'm Ms. A.M.E. Zion because I really enjoy all aspects of the church—on the local level, district level, and a general level. I get joy out of serving the Lord, but you have to enjoy the church in order to do that as well.

My husband is very strong on building rapport. That is very important to him. That way we, as a team, have a good rapport with the congregation, and then you get more out of the people. My husband expects me to be an example for the other women. Also as a deaconess (I was consecrated a deaconess in 1985), we are to be the models for the other women in the church. We try to be those models not just for the younger women but for all the women in the church.

As a pastor's wife, I find it hard to have friends in the church. When I go to a new church as the pastor's wife, I don't go in looking for friends. I want to be friendly, to be able to work with them, to be a model, to be a mentor, to be a supporter and encourage them; but I don't look for women in the church to be in my group of friends. I'm a very private person, and I think that it's just best that people are not into my personal, private life in the church.

I make it a point that I don't invite a lot of church people to my home. Not that I have anything to hide or anything of that nature, but I think there has to be a line somewhere. It's not a line of "I'm better than them," but just a line.

When I go to church, that respect has to be there for the leadership. I think sometimes if you're too familiar with people you lose that level of respect. We may share lunch; we'll get together. It's nice and cordial. We may go out to dinner, but other than that, it's not a thing where we're going to hang together, or we're going to vacation together.

I said to my husband, when he went to Metropolitan, I don't want to be president of a missionary society because I'm the pastor's wife. I'm a leader, but I'm a leader because I can follow. I didn't want to go in and be the leader of women with whom I had no experience. I can't lead if I don't know what you need. And so, let someone be the leader who has been here with the women, who know the women.

There are a lot of things I don't do simply because I am the pastor's wife. It's really hard for a pastor's wife when you feel like you have to suppress your gifts when you know you can do more. When you go into the church, people really don't want you to come in and start doing a lot of stuff. I had to learn that going from the first pastorate until now. It's kind of like when you get new people into your church—people say that they want new members in the church, but they really don't. They don't because they think somebody's going to take their role or their position.

I am careful about not taking over when there's something I know we [as a congregation] could really be doing a little bit better. There's a way that you have to share ideas because people can easily be turned off by the pastor's wife, which, will in turn, turn them off from the pastor. I hear a lot of people say, "I like the pastor, but the pastor's wife is too bossy" or "If it wasn't for the pastor's wife, he would be fine." So, many times I try to stay in my lane. I have learned that I can really adjust to a lot of different situations. I've learned how to take a back seat when need be. That's not really my personality. I'm not a back-seat person.

Since the age of 30-something, I wanted to wear hats to church, but I didn't feel confident enough to do it. Not that I'm saying that a pastor's wife has to wear a hat because that's that whole stereotype. But I wanted to wear hats. I always tell people, once you start, it's hard to stop. On our first Sunday at Metropolitan, church is out, and one of the women walked up to me and said—now this is my first Sunday at the church, and these were her first remarks to me—"We don't wear hats at Metropolitan." I mean, not "Hello. How are you? I'm Mrs. So-and-So"—just, "We don't wear hats at Metropolitan." It threw me. "Okay, who is this person?" So, I smiled and said to her very cordially, "Well, I do and I will wear a hat every Sunday."

Now, over half of the women at Metropolitan wear hats to church every Sunday and not because I said wear a hat or talked to anybody about hats. They would say, "I like your hat." Then people started going out and buying hats. I had some of the younger girls tell me, "I really want to wear a hat, but I just can't find them." I said, "You haven't found the right hat. Start with something small. Don't try to go out and get some big thing. Start with something small and simple, and go from there."

Another Sunday, I wore some individual eyelashes. Well, the next Sunday, four women came to church with lashes on, and I thought it was the funniest thing. One of the other women came up to me and said, "You know what, you've gotten something started in this church. Now, can you look around? You've got four people sitting up in here with lashes on today." It just says to me that people look at the pastor's wife.

There's an honor in being the pastor's wife. People are going to celebrate you. They're going to honor your birthdays and the holidays and do special things for you and make sure that you're comfortable, particularly at my church. We have some of the best members. They really take care of the pastor and the pastor's wife.

There are always people who talk, and some people will say, "Well, you know, in the meeting when they were discussing what they were going to give you for Christmas or something, some people said, 'Well, that's not enough. Some people said that that's too much. Some people said that that's her job.' Everybody's going to have an opinion. But then when it always comes out, they always give, and I don't think they would give it if they really didn't want to give it. I think that's just all a part of the territory. I know the leadership and service that I give at the church. I help everybody. If you ask me to help with something, no matter what it is, I will help. Even if it's something as small as, "Can you make some tickets for me for something?" or "Can you make a flyer for me?" I don't mind doing those things. If you need me to type something for you, I don't have any problem doing that. If you want me to wash dishes, I will wash dishes in the kitchen.

I'm not a selfish person, but I really work on thinking about other people more. Sometimes I'll get home, and I'll say, "You know what, I don't know why I didn't think about that. Why I didn't do this or say that?" or "I meant to say thank you for this." As the pastor's wife, I think that's what you should do, and people expect it. When you don't do it, that's when people think you think that you really deserve this, and that's when people get that negative attitude.

As I said earlier, I hear a lot of that. "Well, I don't like this pastor because I don't like the pastor's wife" or "We want the pastor to come, but we hope he leaves the wife at home." "The wife's a witch, but the pastor is nice." You have to get a feel for the people that you're around. I try to go around and shake hands and speak with people. You can't speak to everyone, but at least you can touch a good number of people so that they don't think you just come to church and you take your seat and then in the end you quickly exit. I think that helps to build rapport in the church where people work with your husband better when they feel comfortable with the wife.

CHAPTER 14

VANESSA OLIVER WARD

Married to the Rev. Dr. Daryl Ward
Omega Missionary Baptist Church
Dayton, OH
Interview Date: August 30, 2008

"I know God called me to preach and to pastoral leadership. I know more today than I even knew six months ago, and it really became solidified four years ago when Daryl became ill."

Pastors' wives serving as co-pastors are a recent phenomenon, and sometimes it's looked upon with skepticism. Vanessa had exercised her leadership ability in various roles in the church and served as the founder and president of the Omega School of Excellence—a charter school in Dayton, OH. She assumed the role of co-pastor shortly before her husband, Daryl fell deathly ill. Through this experience, not only was her faith walk challenged and strengthen, but she felt her call to ministry and pastoral leadership was confirmed by God.

My husband was so accepting of my calling to ministry. I think he knew that I was struggling with this over time because I did not accept my call to the ministry until six years after I started seminary. When I went to seminary, I felt called to a teaching ministry. I had already formed in my mind how I was going to do ministry. It certainly was not to be a pastor. It certainly was not to be someone in the pulpit preaching. I planned to develop Christian education programs, which is one of the first roles that I had at the church. I was the director of Christian education. Daryl was confident and comfortable with that, but I think he saw in me that there was much more to my calling even before I said yes.

Marriage and ministry have been good, but it's been difficult, too. I've seen horrible models. I've seen what I don't want to be, and that's been helpful. I don't want to be the pastor's wife that seems to be put up in that position but hasn't earned it or who the people side with against the pastor. I also want to be his wife, so I am always asking the Lord how do I do that and not compromise what You have called me to do? Knowing sometimes when not to say anything and when to offer suggestions. It's gotten better as I've gotten older and more mature and more confident in myself and in the calling that God has placed on my life.

I know God called me to preach and to pastoral leadership. I know more today than I even knew six months ago, and it really became solidified four years ago when Daryl became ill.

Daryl's illness was one of the hardest things I've ever gone through. It was on December 28, 2004. He came to a staff meeting 45 minutes late and was very much disoriented. He was skipping places in the agenda, and it was very apparent to all of us that something was going on. I said let's go by and see your doctor. At that point, I wasn't thinking major illness.

So, we drove to the doctor's office. The doctor took his blood pressure and said, "It's really elevated and I'm going to admit you to the hospital." We walked out of that doctor's office, and he walked into the hospital. I keep making emphasis to this because what happened after that is just unbelievable. Hour after hour, he became more and more weakened so that by the end of the day, he was not walking. He couldn't use his arms. He just became weaker and weaker.

After their first preliminary tests, they were pretty much convinced that he had had a stroke. After a stroke, you begin to get better and whatever issues you're going to have will kind of make themselves revealed after a couple of days. But instead of that happening, he got worse. So, then they began to question, "Is this really a stroke?" They did several MRIs and saw lesions on his brain that looked like stroke lesions, but it wasn't behaving like it after time went on.

There were still a good number of people who were on the neurological team believing that it was a stroke. There was only one, his main doctor, who was saying this may be something else. And then somebody finally said, one of the neurologists, maybe it's a tumor. They did probably two other MRIs. Both indicated that the lesions were there, and there was a really big mass of lesion or something at the stem of his brain. At that point, they couldn't determine if it was just some type of inflammation, a tumor, or a stroke. By the twelfth day, he had lost so much weight, and he was having fevers.

To me, he was looking like he was nearing death, and there were moments when I actually started trying to prepare myself for what happens if he dies. I've always been a person who has gotten through storms of life being very rational. There's a degree of maturity there, but there's also a degree of just plain old survival mechanism.

On the Martin Luther King Day march, he was so bad, and I remember saying to the chairman of the deacon board, "I think we're losing him." I was really afraid. I was talking to the Lord in a really selfish way, saying, "It's not time, it can't be. Our kids need their father. I need my husband."

I started thinking, we've had a really good life, and if that's what its' supposed to be, then I have to be okay with that, too. We've traveled around the world. We've started several schools in Ghana, West Africa. I mean, who would have thought? You've had 24 years of a wonderful life with a wonderful husband who loved you. You've gotten to do really wonderful things that most people would have never seen—I certainly hadn't seen in my family, the years that I had grown up in Columbus. I'm okay, Lord, if this is it.

I never had those conversations with my kids. The whole time I talked to them about just praying. The kids' support was just incredible through the process. I mean they were praying. They were strong. They worked together with each other. I haven't talked to them about this, and I probably should to find out what conversations they had together because they seemed to be a strong force whenever they were in the hospital. Whenever they went into the room, they just talked to their dad, even when he wasn't responding.

He was losing everything day by day, and he stopped talking. I remember one day he was trying to eat. This was like the fourth day he was in the hospital, and he had started losing his ability to swallow. It was so scary for him that he began to weep. I just kept saying, "It's going to be okay, Daryl. It's going to be okay." But you could tell that he was fearful, too. A couple of days later, he just became totally non-responsive. The kids would come into the room and still talk to him as if he was with us. We needed to assure him that it's going to be okay.

But it just got worse, I guess it was the fifteenth day when the neurologist said after the third MRI that he believed it was a mass. And if it were a mass, he said it's inoperable. He started weeping and said, "I'm really sorry." My sister-in-law was there at the time; we held each other and said we're not giving up. The Lord hasn't said no yet. It's not over until God says it's over.

That neurologist called a very good colleague of his who was over the neurology department at Cleveland Clinic to see if he would take the case because they could determine if it was a mass or what we were dealing with. He called him, and the guy accepted the case the next day. So, we flew to Cleveland.

We got there, and Daryl was supposed to be flown in that afternoon. It turned out, they didn't release the bed at Cleveland Clinic that day, so he had to stay over another day. In the meantime, I got a call from his doctor, he is also a friend of the family, and he tells me, "Now don't panic, but he is really having trouble with his breathing, and I want to put him on a resuscitator. I think he is breathing, but he's just not doing it enough on his own." I said, "Oh, my God! It just kept getting worse.

We had another physician in the church that called me and said, "I'm here with him, and I think it's the right thing." I mean everybody was just talking to me from a distance, and it was wonderful because we had people who I had confidence in who were professionals who kept their eyes on it as well. He said, "I will be with him." They couldn't determine whether it would be a day or two days when they would bring him. So, I drove back with the kids, my mom, and the whole family through a snowstorm and got back to Dayton the very next day. He was in ICU at that point on the respirator.

God just sent angels all through it. I mean, it was just amazing. People from all over the country were calling and saying, "We're praying." Though it was really difficult, I felt God's hand, God's arms around me through every step of it, even in my most fearful moments. He would send a person, or He would send a word. I was also journaling through that process, and I'd journal every day, and it was part of my time with God.

I went into the chapel at Cleveland Clinic once we got there, everyday, and got on my knees and prayed and wrote and prayed and wrote. The journal is very personal, but it actually conveys a lot of the feelings I had. I'm not going to say every day I was hopeful and thankful and encouraged. There were days where I really was struggling. I think God allowed me to struggle with them because it was part of my journey with Him.

I asked questions like, "What happens when I don't have a husband?" Even about sexuality: I'm too young—and the guilt about the times that I didn't receive my husband. And now, you know, dang, you don't have one. I mean those were very real. Those were some very humorous moments and also some difficult moments. Difficult was my birthday, and he wasn't there. Most difficult was that I lost my friend that I talked to about everything.

I mean, we talked about everything, and I had lost that voice. That was really hard.

He was hospitalized for 115 days. Only the last 45 days he was talking. Mostly 80 days were pretty touch-and-go. Even when he left Cleveland Clinic, the realization when they put him in the ambulance to bring him back, they could not bring him back to a hospital. Then he had to go to a nursing home. That was hard. And then to hear them say he's quadriplegic.

Eventually, they determined it was inflammation on the brain. This attacked his brain; his autoimmune system was kind of reversing on itself. They just could not have determined an origin for this. To get him up when he wasn't really able to get up, they had to hold him to get him and harness him to get him standing and moving. It took weeks before he stood and weeks before he took a step, and he had to learn to speak again. We saw his body wake up again.

I probably exhaled about nine months ago. The rehab process was really difficult. It's been three years of really, really hard stuff. It took awhile to get his brain moving. I'd say probably the last nine months, I've seen more of my husband than I'd ever seen over the course of this time. So, while I was breathing, I don't know that I took a deep breath. It was a shallow breathing because at any moment I didn't know what to expect.

Daryl is a miracle walking. I mean there are some parts of him that are different and personality kinds of things that they told me to expect, and that's been hard. It's like getting to know a new person sometimes. But for the most part, I'm really grateful, thankful. He's still my best friend. I still like hanging out with him. I'm thankful.

I think God needed to make Himself even clearer to me, to show Himself to me in a way that gave me confidence in my preaching, teaching, and ministering. I think it takes those personal experiences with the Lord where you know without a shadow of a doubt that there was nobody else but God. I know that I'm called; it confirmed my calling. There's nothing that I won't do for the Lord now. There's nothing that I won't do without Him—no task without calling on Him, no task without conversing with God first. It's changed how I do ministry in a way that I really consult God first. I don't look at anything else.

I have a whole other understanding of being compassionate and patient. When I speak to people about faith in the midst of really difficult situations, I don't feel like I have to get a textbook to figure out how to talk about that. I have often felt myself trying to think about that as I went to minister to someone.

I'm going to the hospital. What should I say? I don't do that anymore. I walk into the hospital confident that God's going to tell me how to do it. I ask God before I walk in to direct me how He want me to speak, what He want me to say. I do that for everything I do because I trust God that much. It's not just a textbook answer. It's not a patent answer. It's what I know. I know it because God did bring me through it. God has kept me with the sane mind through all of this, and He's ordered my life.

God showed favor through it all. Through all of that, we had no financial issues. My husband did not feel any pain, even though it looked like it was a heck of a lot of pain. I didn't merit this experience, but God chose me. And He chose us because He had us in a certain position.

We were high-profile in Dayton, Ohio, not that we're so great, but people knew of Omega. People knew of Pastor Ward. They knew of his wife. They knew of the growth that had gone on in the church. They knew of a church that seemed to be the happening church in many respects. And then they needed to know what people who have that kind of favor do when stuff gets tough.

It's almost like a Job experience, not that I consider myself so righteous. Definitely not, the exact opposite. But what do you do when you're someone who people look up to? How do you walk your faith? I said I wanted to be used by God. I don't know that I quite thought that I was signing up for this, but I'm grateful for the journey.

CHAPTER 15

WANDA TAYLOR-SMITH

Married to the Rev. Dr. Robert Smith
Formerly of New Mission Missionary Baptist Church
Cincinnati, OH
Interview Date: December 28, 2004

*"If you're only going to be yourself, as where you are right
now, then you'll never grow."*

*Despite the fact that Wanda initially did not want to marry Robert, a preacher
and pastor, the two married in 1986, a second marriage for both. He was a
widower and she was a divorcee. In addition to blending a family, Wanda also
had to get out of her comfort zone as she navigated the role of pastor's wife.
While most pastors' wives have advised other pastors' wives to "be yourself,"
Wanda offers a different perspective about the positive outcome one can enjoy
when she is open to not being herself.*

I'm a person who likes to know. Often God will let me know what
lies ahead. When it came to marrying Robert, God said to me,
"This is the man." At the time, my response was, "I don't think so.
That is a preacher, and I don't date preachers."

Having been close to people in the ministry, and knowing what
they have gone through, marrying a preacher was not my cup of
tea. When he brought marriage up, I told him, "I don't know about
all this. I don't think I want to do this." I had no plans of ever
getting married again and certainly was not getting married to a
preacher.

I said, "I have to know if I can stand to hear you preach
because if I can't stand to hear you preach, I know God and I
are going to have to discuss this a little further." So, I attended a

service to specifically experience his preaching. My conclusion was, "Hmm, he does pretty good. I think I can listen to this man." I am still fascinated by his preaching.

In becoming the wife of a pastor, I knew I would have to come out of my shell. I am an introvert. I'm not a touchy-feely person, and some people expect that of you. Everybody does not have to change to accommodate that, but it came to me that God had to deal with me in that area. God's message to me was, "It's not about you. I didn't bring you to this point just for you to have fun or for you to do your own thing. You're here for a reason, and this is what you're to do."

We decided that he was going to announce our engagement one Sunday after morning service. At the end of the service, he asked me to come to the front of the church with the children. He presented me as his future wife. Much commotion followed. I asked Bobby, our oldest son, who was standing next to me, please not to move because I was holding on to him for dear life as the congregation surged forth to greet us.

We subsequently had an open forum with the Pastor's Aide Ministry so the people could get to know me and feel more comfortable around me. I am not sure that it helped. One of the questions that came up was when was I going to join the church? I said, "I don't know, whenever the Lord tells me." They said, "Oh." I think they may have thought I considered myself "above" him.

The Marshalls of First Baptist Church of Oakley, who were my pastor and pastor's wife at the time, were like second parents to me. I played the piano for the senior choir and the children's choir. The church was like family to me. Leaving them would mean that they had to find somebody else to play, and that was one of the problems. So, we had to work through that. I did eventually join Robert's church after about six months.

When we first got married, I had to subtly establish some boundaries. The church members were so used to him being at their beck and call day and night. The first thing I did that upset some of the folks was "I moved him way out there in Montgomery" (a suburb of Cincinnati). According to the church, "he had no business being way out there," a distance from the church. It was not entirely intentional. We could not live in the two bedroom house I had with a blended family of three boys and one girl because it was too small. I read all the information about blending families, and one of the requirements is to have adequate space. Thus the move was necessary.

Another boundary was when parishioners called, I would determine whether he could be disturbed. If he was busy, I would take a message, or if he was sleeping, I wouldn't wake him up unless there was a dire situation. That got around the church. He had gotten sick one time, and I made an announcement in church that he would not be receiving visitors. They came to the house anyway. The man was almost falling off his chair he was so weak and tired. I had to tell them, "I'm sorry but this isn't a good time."

When I first came to the church, they did not know what to think about me. I'm thinking I am nobody. I am no threat to anybody, what would make them think that? I discovered people thought differently.

There was a lovely couple who called after I had had surgery. I was hungry, and they told me they were fixing hamburgers. When they said they would bring me something to eat, I thought they were going to bring me one of those juicy hamburgers they said that they had just fixed. But when they came, they didn't bring a hamburger. I said, "Where's my hamburger?" They looked at me like they were in total shock. They said, "We didn't bring you a hamburger." I asked, "Why not?" "We didn't think you ate hamburger!" They had gone somewhere and gotten something else. Then I was in shock. I'm thinking who doesn't eat hamburger? They said they thought I was a "steak woman." That has been a joke amongst us since that time.

Some in the congregation may have thought I was trying to take him faster than he needed to be taken. Some people would probably think that if he hadn't married me that he would still be there. They said I was trying to push him beyond where he needed to be. To them, I came along and changed the program, changed him. He started dressing differently. He started doing things differently.

I told him, "You know you have a gift that God is doing something with, and this place is not where you are going to be." He loved to teach. He would have all sorts of classes, but the people did not seem to appreciate it. They wouldn't come to class. He did classes for our children, too. I said, "You need to ease up on these children. You need to find somebody else to teach." It was hilarious. The children didn't think so. I knew that God had given him something that was going to be spread a lot farther than New Mission Missionary Baptist Church. When he did finally leave the pastorate there, some of the people were angry.

I always think of Christians as being ambassadors, as God's representative on earth. People, whom you never know, are watching you. You have to constantly be aware of that fact. I see pastors' wives who are rebellious and say, "I'm just going to be me." Good point. You need to be you, but when "being you" starts to detract from the ministry, from what you could be doing for God and negatively impacting how people see God through you, then there's a problem.

For example, let's say you, as part of a group, are supposed to do a certain thing to show unity. Let's say you are all supposed to wear white in a certain event. You have someone who doesn't want to wear white and refuses to sit in the designated spot. Some people may say, "It's not that important." Well, then if it's not important why wouldn't you want to comply with the group? It shows unity. It shows cooperation. But, more importantly, when you do not do it, then what message are you sending? Another example of "being you": I'm not a preacher, and I can drink if I want. I can smoke if

I want. That's true. Yes, you can. But what does that say about your witness for God. What kind of example are you setting?

I have had to deal with my own issues of rebellion. I did not want to speak publicly. The first time the church asked me to speak at Women's Day, I declined. I said I am not a speaker. But you know what? I got over that. I am not a "huggy-feely" person, and I do not consider myself a warm, fuzzy person. But I had to move beyond that also. It was not so much that people expected it, but they *needed* it. Sometimes people did not get affirmation any place else.

A woman once told me nobody had hugged her in seven years. I could not believe it! What if I had refused to hug this woman? Or, if I had said, "Oh, I don't hug people." That would have been selfish. A hug was a gift that I had that I could give to her. If there is anything you can do for somebody that is going to be helpful and positive, and if it is not going to hurt you, do it.

I have changed some things about how I dress not because I am a preacher's wife but because I do not want to be a stumbling block to anybody. I do not want to present myself in a manner that would be negative or bring dishonor to God.

Before we were married, the church had a fashion show in which I wore a rather clingy dress. It caused quite a stir. After we got married, I didn't wear that type of attire anymore. On our first anniversary, the color scheme was gold along with another color. I had borrowed a dress that was low in the front, so I added a piece of lace across the front to avoid any trouble. But the dress caused a stir not because it was low but because it was gold!

The latest thing I did that was questioned was that I wore some red shoes with ankle straps to church. The content of the conversation after church was about "those shoes!" People did not say it directly, but it was as if, "You are not supposed to have on those shoes." Had I not been married to the pastor and wore those shoes, I do not think anybody would have said anything. People come in the church with all kinds of things on, and no one says anything to them. Both men and women were talking about these shoes, so I decided that I would not wear those shoes to church again. I have worn the shoes elsewhere, and no one had that kind of response. I try not to draw unnecessary negative attention.

My husband wanted me to wear hats, even though he knew I was not a hat person. It's not such a big deal. He's not a demanding person, but he wanted me to wear a hat. I can do that. It has to do with how you look at marriage and how you regard your mate. I believe that you are supposed to try to please them and make them happy as long as the request is nothing really outrageous. It's not hurting me to wear a hat. However, there are some things you should not do because it compromises who you are as a person and as a Christian. I believe you have to choose your battles based on biblical principles.

My conversations with God helped me to realize that this walk is not about me. You are here for a reason; you are here for a purpose. I have no doubt that I have been put here in this particular place at this particular time for whatever purpose God has for me. I think God deals with you on the level that is specific to your personality and understanding. If you are only going to be yourself, as where you are right now, then you will never grow. You will never experience anything because all you are going to do is what you are already doing.

There are times when visiting the sick, my husband will say, "I'm going to ask you to pray when we go in, would you mind?" That took some growth also. The first time he did that, I thought, "Pray in public!? Oh my gosh! You want me to have an absolute heart attack?" Then I did a class on prayer that helped me to understand what prayer is and that, as a Christian, you should be able to pray. I had to get over being self-conscious and fearful about not knowing what to say or that I would use the word wrong or say something amiss. God said to me,

"You are not praying to these people. Even if they are critical you're still not praying to them." I got better; it got better.

It is vital that you keep your relationship with God fresh and open. Get as close as you can to God through prayer. Learn as much as you can by reading His word, the Bible. Be open to God's will because as long as you hold onto "you," greater things cannot happen. It is that fear of letting go, of no longer being you. Trust God with "you."

Who am I? I am who God is shaping me to be. This is no longer "me." That can be a good thing because you cannot grow unless there is some kind of change. I would not be where I am in my spiritual growth had I not married Robert because I would not have been exposed to all of these opportunities to grow. It's a good thing.

CHAPTER 16

RHONDA GILLESPIE RANEY
Widow of The Rev. G. Wesley Raney
Macedonia New Life Church
Raleigh, NC
Interview date: July 1, 2008

**"The hard part about [relinquishing the role of first lady]
was the connection between that and the fact that my husband is no longer here, not so much the role itself."**

*Walking through the death of a husband is difficult for any woman. But when
a pastor dies, many scenarios could play out. For Rhonda, not only did she have
to deal with her own grief, she also took on the role of comforting a mourning
church, providing a stable physical presence for a church in transition, and
providing a bridge between her husband and the next servant leader.*

Wesley had this little cough that was more like the sound you
make when your airflow is being interrupted. He'd gone
to the doctor, and they determined that is was bronchitis or some
respiratory issue. He had gotten some medication for it, and it
would sort of get better. Then it came back again not long after
the initial onset. It had gotten to the place where when he was
preaching he would be interrupted because it would be like his
airflow would be cut off. I insisted that he go back to the doctor to
check this out.

They did x-rays and then referred him to another physician,
and that's when they found a spot on his lung. He was diagnosed
with stage four lung cancer. Wesley was not a smoker and had
never been, so the lung cancer diagnosis took us completely by sur-
prise. We decided we were going to trust God. We knew that God

heals in time and in eternity, and until He made it absolutely clear which one it would be, we were going to claim healing in time.

Wesley decided that he did not want to do the traditional therapy (radiation and chemotherapy) because of the havoc that it could wreak on the body. He would allow God's provision to be the medicine, and that being the Word of God and natural remedies. He had a homeopathic physician. Consequently, he was able to lead a tremendously strong quality of life and was able to work and preach and continue to function. He insisted on living life as normally as we could within the context of his illness. He was never confined to the bed except for maybe the last two weeks.

When he was very ill—he had been out of the pulpit about eight weeks—he said, "I want to go to church." That morning he was very weak but very independent, very strong. The week before we were planning to go to church, I had taken one of his suits to be altered because he had lost a lot of weight. I really wanted him to feel as good as he could feel about going.

That morning I picked out his tie, and he said, "I don't want to wear this tie. Give me another tie." I said, "We don't have time to pick another tie." Then he said, "Come here, James. We need to do our tie-tying lesson again." My son had always worn ties, but he never knew how to tie them, so they had started these tie-tying lessons, but he hadn't had one in a while. And I said, "We've got to go. We don't have time for tie-tying lessons."

Then he told me, "Let me have a shaver because you got my lines wrong." He was very meticulous about his appearance, and I had gotten a line a little crooked on his mustache. I was just amazed at how much time we're taking, and let alone I hadn't figured out how we're going to get to the car.

We made it to the car and to church. He was only going to sit for a little while. When he said he was ready to go, I got the guys to help him. They were going to follow me home to help me get him back in the house. I had driven the car around front, up on the sidewalk and right at the doors at the front entrance of the church, and I waiting, and I asked, "What is taking them so long?" He was sitting in the back of the church, and we're at the front doors of the church just looking down, and he just didn't want to go yet. I believe he probably knew that that might be his last time there, at least for some significant period of time.

I continued to go to work for a couple hours a day. I'd get up in the morning, get his breakfast ready, do the body cleanup, and get everything squared away. My sister-in-law was here, and so she would stay with him, and I would go to work maybe until about noon and then come back for the rest of the day. That morning, I woke up and the Lord very clearly spoke to me and said, "Don't go today." So, I called my office and said I wouldn't be coming in that day.

We had a chance to have a longer devotion. Then he got sleepy and went to sleep, and I went outside to paint some antique wicker chairs. My sister-in-law came to the door and said, "Rhonda, come here!"

He was lying in bed, and he was tossing and turning as if he was in this physical struggle. It was almost like he was boxing. I woke him up and said, "Are you okay?" "Yeah, I'm okay." It was as if he was clearly conscious and clearly listening to me because he could hear me to respond, but at the same time there was something else going on. I later decided that God was saying, "It's time for you to come home." And he was saying, "I can't do it. I've got some things I need to do." It was clearly just very unusual.

He settled down and said, "I think I'll take a nap." So, I took a shower and then came back out and just sat by his bed. Eventually, he stopped breathing, and I performed CPR on him. There were clear "no resuscitation" orders, but I just had to do that. At that point, I knew that day was his last. That's why the Lord had me be home.

He breathed on his own for about another hour. When he stopped breathing again, I didn't do anything. I didn't call anyone immediately because I just said, "Okay, Lord. You raised Lazarus, so

I'm just going to lie here until you tell me it's time to get up." So, for an hour and a half, I just lay on his shoulder and went to sleep. I woke up, and the Lord said, "Okay."

It was very difficult going back to church because I knew he was never going to come back. It was easier going while he was ill. I continued to go while he was sick because he was not in need of constant care.

My time at church at that point was going to the 11:00 service and then back home. There was not a lot of lag time afterwards. Going to church was for me as much as it was for the parishioners because they got strength seeing me come every week. That was their sign that I was well. I later came to appreciate it more because people would tell me that just my being there said that he's not so bad that she couldn't come away and leave him. I would go to Bible study. I never really stopped anything because, at that point, he was basically taking a sabbatical to conserve his energy, be in prayer, and just let the Lord do His work.

So, coming back afterwards was difficult. There were times when I couldn't sit through the whole service, and I would leave. It was difficult because so much of our lives [together] was church.

There were several Sundays I did not want to go, but I knew that that's what I needed. I became more conscious that's what the people needed. People would say, "The only reason why I'm here is because you're here." The people were in mourning. That relationship [between pastor and congregation] is a very special one, and when the relationship works, to lose someone to death is very hard for people to get over. My husband wasn't the generic sort of pastor; he had such a personal relationship with everybody.

It wasn't just a situation where you were between pastors, but also you had people who were dealing with loss. We're also talking about a church in transition, and what role do I play in this transition in preparing it to be turned over to the next servant? I became more and more aware that was my job. I sort of became the voice for G. Wesley Raney: What was he thinking?

I decided that I was going to be limited [in some areas], and in others I wanted to be more active. Mostly at that point, though, my attention was turned inward, just trying to manage for myself and my son and being a physical presence for people who needed the physical presence. I don't believe that my assignment is Macedonia for an indefinite period of time. I am on assignment now, and I believe that the Lord will be very clear when He is ready to release me.

The hard part about [relinquishing the role of first lady] was the connection between that and the fact that my husband is no longer here, not so much the role itself. There's nothing about the title, the role, or being first in the line that I miss. I'm not trying to operate in that role because I recognize that that's not my role [anymore]. I very much saw it as my responsibility and my job to try to show as much support for the new family coming in so that people could see that I am comfortable with this, so you can be comfortable, too.

When I remarried, the pastor was very helpful in that transition. He said, "Her vows were "Til death do us part.' G. Wesley Raney is with the Lord, and she's got to live her life. So, before you start thinking it is okay for you to go home to your husband and for her to have to go home by herself, 'She's ours! She belongs to us! We'll take care of her!' Think again! That's selfish. That's not God's way." He really made some comments that were probably very helpful to some people. It was another reality check that G. Wesley Raney is gone.

My husband has been great. You have to be a confident person in order to come in behind anybody. He knows G. Wesley Raney III is going to always live in all of our lives, and he doesn't fight that. He recognizes that because he lived in all of our lives, all of us are better, stronger. He's smart enough and self-confident enough to understand that he's not competing with anyone. So, there are pictures of Wesley downstairs on the mantle that he's good with; he understands.

I have a son, and there's no erasing anything. I'm still Rhonda Raney. I didn't change my name, so I still am Rhonda Raney. Every year, we have the G. Wesley Raney III Walk for Prostate Cancer Awareness, and now my husband is on the committee. It's just the healthiest, smoothest transition that I can imagine. God is just good.

God's provision kept being more evident. I knew that there was a reason that He called Wesley so early. I knew that His plan was greater than mine and that His wisdom far exceeded my own. We weren't married that long, but what we had in quality far exceeded maybe what somebody else might have been able to get in 50 years of married life, and 40 of them were miserable.

I couldn't find anything that I needed to be angry about. I felt plenty that I could be sad about in terms of what I was missing. But looking at it from a fairness or an equity perspective, I couldn't blame God. He had given me so much, and it was such good quality. Not perfect; nobody has a perfect marriage. If I was the person of faith that I claimed to be, then I needed to understand that He takes care of all and consequently would take care of me and my son. It was time to put my walk where my mouth was.

I've got to rely on God who is able to do exceedingly and abundantly above all that we can ever imagine. It comes out of the book and off the page and becomes a reality. I wouldn't be any more prepared to do it again, except relying on the same source day after day after day. It was an incredible faith experience.

106

CHAPTER 17

TERRI SUTTON

Married to the Rev. Al B. Sutton, Jr.
Sixth Avenue Baptist Church
Birmingham, AL
Interview Date: July 29, 2008

"I noticed it was an entirely different ball game at our installation when they didn't have a seat for me."

It's a blessing when a pastor's wife is blessed by, connects with and enjoys the church her husband pastors. But, what does she do, when she feels like an outsider? Or that her husband has been disrespected? Despite that fact that a small minority of people in Terri's historic and elite congregation have made her feel excluded, she has learned to encourage her husband and children, while accepting difference between she and the congregation.

My priority is Terri. When I'm 90 years old and I look back on my life, I want to say that I was true to myself. I did what I wanted and, most importantly, what Terri needed, not in a selfish manner but that I lived my life to the fullest because God gave me this life, one life, and to honor me would be to honor Him. I must be true to *that* individual.

Second, I am a wife. And as anyone who has ever been married can attest, it's *hard* work. Daily. It is during good times, challenging times, and times of doubt that I refer to Ephesians 5:25: "For husbands, this means love your wives, just as Christ loved the church. He gave up his life for her." Whether in front of, behind, or in the midst of joy or tribulation, I know that AB Sutton Jr. loves God and unequivocally loves me.

We are parents. God entrusted us with a life times three. We were young and inexperienced, yet nurture and care instinctively became second nature. Being a mom has caused a state of euphoria that I could never otherwise imagine. The love that I have for my children from the moment we met is indescribable. The serenity that exudes our family time is unmatched. Unabashed, so often, due to my husband's busy schedule, the children are all I have, and that is okay with me.

Last, would be the church. I'm currently serving in my second church as a pastor's wife. In this ever-evolving role as first lady, there was always a subconscious yet constant, gentle force reminding me to always protect my family. Our first church was a small, loving congregation. The faithful few worked hard, and their contributions and presence were appreciated and direly missed if ever absent.

Unlike our second church, Sixth Avenue, which was also a loving congregation; however, their focus was neither pastor-driven nor first family-orientated. That "isolation," however, allowed me the opportunity to be a pew member and to raise my children full-time. Because once again, my husband was working nonstop, and I was in a new town with small children and no family within 300 miles. The larger congregation lead to a greater opportunity to be overlooked and, hence, allowed me to melt into the background.

One of the few silent expectations was that I wear a yellow collar and all white on the first Sundays. It's been eight years, and no one has ever given me a collar. It was an unspoken assumption that I would simply follow suit. I never did, not out of defiance or protest. I just plainly didn't see the purpose of it. Why would you go and sit and do nothing and have no purpose? Some others would probably say, "Be supportive. It's the culture of the church. The church is over 100 years old. They've been doing it this this way for a very long time." But they don't serve Communion or do anything on first Sundays. They just sit there. I can't.

We officially arrived in Alabama in August. That fall, during the holiday season, literally every weekend, there were two to three black-tie functions, which the pastor and wife were expected to attend. It's a socialite church, high society. But, it completely wore us out. Gowns, tuxes, children and babysitters became our status quo conversation. "If we had one more black-tie function to attend, just shoot me," became my mantra. What is it really all for? Where is the ministry in it all? I realize that there is a necessary social element to society and community; however, let us not replace festive with function and service. Go out into the communities you raise funds for. Meet the people. Embrace them; hear their voices.

I noticed it was an entirely different ball game at our installation when they didn't have a seat for me. They just said, "Go ahead and sit anywhere." It was on that day that I said, "You're not in Kansas anymore. This 'game' has changed for you and the pastor." But once again, I don't need stroking; however, on this day I thought a designated seat was not too much to ask. But they don't have a lot of regard for the pastor, let alone his wife. The overall conscious was, "You should be happy to be here, the pastor of the Sixth Avenue Baptist Church. You should be honored to be in Birmingham."

For me, I'm so resilient that it didn't faze me, but when the lack of respect oscillates toward my husband, the pastor, then we have a problem. In order for a meaningful pastor-congregant connection to be established, it is crucial that the respect for him exists. In fairness, it's not the majority of the congregation, but it's the loud, overpowering minority. It's the group who attends all the meetings, making the most ruckus and causing ultimate chaos.

This minority succeeded in making me feel unwelcomed. I am a New Yorker, for crying out loud. That brash, boisterous stereotype preempted an actual meet-and-greet between myself and some of the congregants. I was "diagnosed" solely based on the state I was birthed in. And that Southern hospitality? Not so much! Not from that minority and not for a Yankee.

109

My approach was to roll with the punches. Remember, I am a Yankee, and my innate capacity to recoil is resounding. I went to all the Christian education classes in order to get to know the membership and to allow them to become acquainted with me. Many in the congregation grew up together. There is a large group in the fellowship that has attended this church for 50+ years. And those members were very proud to share that accomplishment with anyone who would listen. It was a badge of honor to be in that group.

When we first arrived in Birmingham, housing had not been secured. We had been traveling back and forth from New York to Alabama; however, our housing situation was of great concern. We were packed: Two small children, check! One big dog, check! And all my earthly possessions, check! Packed and ready to leave New York with no place to stay.

Upon arrival, we soon found a place that needed plenty of TLC and some cosmetic work. We stayed in a Residence Inn for weeks until the work was complete. It seemed as though the search committee completed its job. They found a pastor, he arrived in the city, job DONE! In hindsight, there should have been a welcoming committee to ensure that the transition was as seamless as possibly.

Once we got here, we were basically on your own. It was as though they said, "We're giving you a salary. You know some people. You know the realtors. Figure it out." However, in their defense, the church was 120 years old; they have had, literally, only one handful of pastors in the entire existence. All of their previous pastors' tenures lasted for decades, and all of them were from Alabama. They simply didn't know how to bring in a new pastor from out of state and from a different church culture.

We rented a home for two years and then decided to build our long-term residence. We needed a construction loan. We were approved at a local bank, but one of the deacons came to us and said why would we go to a bank when the church credit union could finance that loan right here. Great idea, we thought. It's a no brainer. We're paying our own mortgage, why not pay "our" credit union. It would not cost the church a dime. As a matter of fact, they can profit from the process. My husband and I didn't see a problem.

A church meeting was called to formally present the arrangement. More people than normal were present for this meeting. I found that to be odd. And that oddity was the intro for a most challenging night.

"We're not buying you a house!" "I bought my house. You buy your house," were some of the comments that sprawled out of the mouths of the ill-informed. There was no convincing them that they weren't buying our house. They were merely giving us financing, costing the church nothing. At the end of a very long meeting, financing was finally granted, and I was forever marred. My husband being the epitome of unblemished optimism says, "In the end, we got what we wanted, financing, so you should be happy." That is why I love him forever and a day. With the love of God, he balances me, who balances us.

As a wife, the most difficult thing I've seen my husband go through is probably wanting to move to the next level and forced into stagnation because of the bureaucracy. The church will have a meeting before the meeting to establish a subcommittee meeting to determine when to meet again. In the interim, your issues may not survive the journey.

Through each tumultuous and/or harmonious event, I had to be the example for my children. I don't want them to grow up hating the church so much that they stop attending and become victims of the streets. So many PK's (preacher's kids) have spiritually struggled due to the church. Through the grace of God, I am able to protect my children, but it remains my constant prayer. I pray not to give them a false sense of reality or of human nature.

When I was blissfully glowing and pregnant with our third child, I lost the baby. Stillborn at eight months. The church was so supportive. Their innate ability to express overwhelming love and concern warms my heart to this day. There were some awesome people with generous and sincere hearts as big as the moon. Sometimes injured persons can become lost and frozen in that space. We (my husband and I) refuse to be those people. I implore you not to get stuck in the hurt.

I know now that people are different. Just because they're different doesn't make them wrong or malicious nor does it make them right. They're just different, and I've learned to accept those differences. This thing called life and lessons learned has been quit a trek. But like the songwriter says, "I wouldn't take nothing for my journey now, come too far to turn around."

CHAPTER 18

JUDITH HAYES DAVIS

Married to The Rev. Frederick Davis
First Calvary Baptist Church
Durham, NC
Interview Date: July 2, 2008

"I try to be the wife that my husband needs me to be and not so much what a position expects me to be. If God is satisfied and if Fred is satisfied, then whatever else everybody else thinks doesn't matter."

Judy married Fred when they had both recently graduated from college and were in their early twenties. She not only has matured as a wife and mother, but also in her understanding of ministry and her role in it. Throughout the years, she's gained an understanding that ministry was neither about she nor her husband, but rather glorifying God.

What I really like about Fred is that Fred is Fred. I know some people live double lives. They live one way in church and another when they get home. Fred is the same way in the pulpit as he is when he's talking with somebody else.

I think the success of our marriage is probably more him than it is me because he's easy to love because he's easy to follow because he's really authentic. I think that's why people appreciate him because what you see is what you get all the time. I admire that. He's funny. He laughs. He jokes. He doesn't cause people to feel uncomfortable. If you put yourself in an unreachable position, then how do you really reach the people?

I think I'm really accessible, too. I've had people say that I'll just talk to anybody. I've had even young people say, "Our pastor's wife wouldn't talk. It was like she was there, but she felt like she had to be on this pedestal."

I think it's my job; I have the gift of helps. I've heard people say, "You don't look like… You don't act like a pastor's wife." I always say, "Well probably not, because I'm not really a pastor's wife, I'm Fred's wife." We grew up together, so I didn't really have to try to fit into a mold, and he never really required me to do that. When I look at my role as being a pastor's wife, I really look at it as being Fred's wife, so it's never really been cumbersome.

Fred was at ITC [Interdenominational Theological Center] and was looking at the board, and there was a flyer from this little church in Lanett, Alabama. He went down and did a trial sermon, and they called him to be pastor. We were 24 and 25. I always tell people I think God decided to send us there because we were young and in love, so it really wouldn't matter. But if I had to go back now, oh God, I'd die! It was really country. The grand dragon of the KKK lived about 20 miles down the road.

I really thought that perhaps for Fred it was a job. It was a divine job, but it was a job. In Alabama, he'd get these preaching engagements, he'd travel 30 miles, and maybe they'd give him $20. I was thinking, "My husband has a Master's degree, and you're giving him $20?" My mom would say, "Judy, just close your mouth!" And I would say, "Oh, man!" He was okay with it.

People would call and say, "Pastor, how much do you charge for your revivals?" He'd say, "Anything you want to give." When we were down in Lanett in 1982, they were paying Fred $150 a week. During the wintertime, the gas bill was on an average of $300 to $350 because the house was not well insulated. You had to run the heat around the clock because once you cut it off, it felt like subzero weather.

It's funny now. Those were the times that really make you understand that there is a God. I learned how to make spaghetti sauce out of ketchup. I wouldn't take anything for it now. Even

114

when I look back on it, I was never, ever unhappy. I realized that God is God, and God can do. Obedience is better than sacrifice. I realized God is really the owner of everything, and he shall supply. We never went hungry, we never went lacking, even when the money wasn't in the bank, God never failed.

When the $350 gas bill came, we didn't know that it was a tradition that they paid the visiting evangelist, and they also gave the pastor a little stipend for carrying him around and feeding him or whatever, and that was like $350. Fred said, "Judy, you won't believe this!" We had gotten the bill earlier that day not knowing that later on that night they were going to give him the stipend. And you know what he did then? He said, "Oh, no! I can't take this!" And then one of the deacons said, "Pastor, that's our tradition. Would you please?" I think he has always known that it really wasn't about him, but it took me a while to understand that God is going to provide whether man does his part or not. If you're faithful, he will do it.

Even though he's a pastor, Fred feels like his job as pastor is to affect what goes on in the community because people don't live in the church. When he called me and said he was going to run for a school board, I said, "Yeah," because I figured he wouldn't win. Then when it started to look like it was becoming a reality, I said, "Oh." And my mom said, "Like he needs something else to do." And I said, "Yeah." But I think that he does make a difference.

The real challenge was trying to navigate three boys when he was away. When I look at it, I thank God for the kind of insulation that he did give me. The boys are five years apart, and so that means sometimes it was high school, middle school, and elementary school. You are a single parent for a week when you're used to somebody being there. Even if they're not always there, you know they're in town, and if you need them you can call them.

We've never lived in a place where we have family. It is important if your husband is a pastor that you have that family support. I marvel at how God sent people in our lives. I really didn't want to come to Durham; I had gotten comfortable in Huntsville. I said, "God, please send me a friend." No sooner than I had prayed for that, God sent me somebody. They had two sons who were close in age, and we had similar likes.

People say teachers' and pastors' children are the worst. And I said, "Yeah, that's so because we're always trying to take care of somebody else's." With our schedules, we sometimes, unfortunately, neglect our own. I promised God that if He gave me three sons, three black boys in America, they are going to need somebody's attention. I understood Fred's position in the community and in the church, and so a lot of times he was absent, but he was supportive. I had to be the mainstay.

Among the gifts that God gives, I think I have the gift of parenting. I just took it very, very serious. I said, "God, if you've given them to me, to us, I'm going to guard them." I know Fred is covering them, but he can't be here all the time. So, I just really made a concerted effort for a couple of years just to be in place and not try to make every meeting or whatever because I think my first role, even as a pastor's wife, is to make sure that the pastor's home and his children are taken care of.

When I came to Durham, I said, "God, I don't want to come here." I remember when the moving van was in front of the house in Huntsville, I said, "God, you can do anything. You can move this moving van. You can change things around, and we can just stay here. Fred's going to be busy. Why did do I have to come here? God, in your own time, I know you're going to answer me because you always do, but I just want to know why I had to come here." About my eighth month in Durham, I was sitting in church, and about seven or eight people came to accept Christ—a variety of boys and girls and adults. And the Spirit of God said, "Is moving to Durham, North Carolina, too much to ask so that men, women, boys, and girls might be saved?" It was just like a floodgate of tears. I just kept saying, "No. That's not."

I've matured in understanding what this is about. It's never about us. This is all about Christ. When you glorify Him, and you do what he asks you to do, everything else will be taken care of. This is not about your creature comforts or about what you like or what you dislike. These are just temporary quarters.

I had gotten really kind of comfortable with my house in Huntsville, and I think God said, "This is not about you getting comfortable with a house on earth because you don't want to stay here, do you?" People ask, "Do you think you're going to stay in Durham?" And I say, "Well, if it's God's will, we'll stay; and if it's not, hey, I'm ready to go." I think that's the real theology that drives what I do and even me being the partner that I am with Fred.

If all of this is really about who we are called to be, then a pastor's wife is not hard at all. I try to be the wife that my husband needs me to be and not so much what a position expects me to be. If God is satisfied and if Fred is satisfied, then whatever else everybody else thinks doesn't matter.

CHAPTER 19

EMELDA TOLBERT

Married to Bishop Mark C. Tolbert
Victorious Life Church
Kansas City, MO
Interview: August 4, 2008

"I think pastors' wives have to be transparent. My son was killed on Friday, and Sunday morning we were in church praising the Lord. When you're going through something, the congregation has to be able to see that you are human, too."

When Emelda married Mark, the second youngest son in a family of ministers, she believed she would probably remain a minister's wife. Little did she know how serving in the capacity of a minister's wife would greatly prepare her to assume the role of first lady. Along the journey, she learned one of the greatest testimonies she could offer was to be transparent with her congregation as she faced illness, loss, and death.

When I met Mark in 1976, he was a young minister, serving in many capacities within the church his father pastored. Actually, I met Mark through his brother, who hired me at the Safeway grocery store where he was a manager. An entrepreneur at heart, Mark also owned and operated his own Smacks Franchise, a very popular hamburger restaurant. He and his brother invited me to visit their church, and after several months of visiting, I joined. A couple of years later, Mark and I got married. To our union, two sons were born, Mark Curtis Jr. and Britton Elliott.

I thought serving in the capacity of a minister's wife would not be too bad. You help with the ministry, but it's not like having the whole gamut. I never thought I would become the first lady of the church.

My husband had two older brothers who were both ministers, and one of them was already pastoring a church in Waterloo, Iowa. I figured one of them would assume the role as pastor upon their father's retirement. A few years later, his other older brother accepted a position with a company and relocated to another state. Shortly afterward, my husband's dad appointed him to the position of co-pastor. At that point, it was evident that he could possibly become the pastor.

My husband and I worked for many years under the pastoral leadership of his father and mother. My husband assisted with preaching, teaching, programming, operations management, and whatever else was needed. Having a background in accounting, a degree in fashion merchandising, and a skillful hand at cooking, I worked in the accounting office, decorated the church, and hosted people in our home. We did it cheerfully, and our service was not to naught.

Great leaders are developed through serving others, for "greatest among you will be he that is a servant." The more preparation and training ministers and ministers' wives can get to help develop them as great servants, it will definitely have an effect on how well they operate in the roles of pastor and first lady. We certainly had our fair share of service duties.

In 1989, my father-in-law announced his retirement and informed the congregation that my husband was one of the candidates for pastor. One of the young ladies in the church approached me and asked, "What would you propose you are going to do as the first lady, because it is evident that your husband is probably going to be the next pastor?' I said to her, "Well, I didn't realize I was on a campaign trail. Furthermore, as the first lady, my biggest responsibility in fulfilling my role will be to take care of my husband so he can take care of God's business." I was a young minister's wife at the time, but I still hold true to that philosophy.

The church voted my husband in as pastor. He and I were both in our early 30's. I came in with the attitude that all I can be is me. I did not come with any airs about myself or the position. I was a little country girl from Louisiana, but the only thing country about me was my accent.

At the installation service I was asked to give remarks. In my closing remarks, I stated, "I can't fill my mother-in-law shoes, so I brought my own with me." This was a staunch Pentecostal church that I did not grow up in. I knew that coming in from Catholicism not knowing anything about Pentecostalism, some of them would probably try and give me a run for my money. Without a doubt, if I came in naïve, intimidated, and insecure, some of them were going to try and run me ragged.

Some people say being a minister's wife and being a pastor's wife is the same. I've been in both roles, and they're quite different. As a minister's wife, you are observed by the people; but as a pastor's wife, you are on a whole new level of not only observation, but scrutiny. As a minister's wife, if you don't show up for something, some may miss you, some may not. As a pastor's wife, if you don't show up, some may say, "Where's the pastor's wife?" A minister's wife can take the attitude that it is not her baby, but a pastor's wife will end up taking on a lot of ownership and responsibility of things because she really wants the ministry to be successful.

I have worn so many hats over the years. I've been a cook, a grocery shopper, an interior decorator, a bookkeeper, an innkeeper, a teacher, a program director, an event planner, an auxiliary leader—and as the song goes, "You Name It."

My husband and I would keep people in our home that were ministering at the church, sometimes five and six people at a time. We were both working full-time jobs outside of ministry and had small children back then. I would get up, go to work, come home and fix meals, serve the guest, go to church, come back home and sometimes wash the preacher's clothes before I went to bed, get up the next day, and do it all over again. But that's a part of the first lady role that people don't see.

When people look at where you are today—the big ministry, the school, and the nice facilities—some may want to be a first lady, but not too many of them will want to make the sacrifice of what it took to get here. They don't have a clue what you have sacrificed to be here. I love people. I love the Lord. I love ministry. In ministry, you have to have a love for it because it is definitely more sacrifice than salary. If you don't have a love for it, if you're not willing to sacrifice for it, it will be a very frustrating role.

You can't try to please people. My slogan as a pastor's wife is "You have to be a friend to all and a buddy to none." I think that is really what has helped me to be able to continue to press forward whether I get the full support of the people or not. Some people are fickle. I just be myself and try to treat people like I want to be treated.

It doesn't matter if I have a welfare mother or a CEO wearing a St. John knit suit waiting to talk to me, I am going to give the same time to that welfare mother as I would to the CEO. I'm a people person and very much approachable.

My husband and I are not the kind of pastor and pastor's wife who head to our office or escape through a back door and get into a chauffeured limousine at the end of service. We stand up front to greet and talk to the congregation and visitors. You would be surprised at the number of members who have my cell phone number. Working in ministry is a very sacrificing profession; however, it also has its rewards of personal fulfillment, unique to any other profession. The church is a lifesaving station, and we are actually saving lives here.

I think pastor's wives have to be transparent, not necessarily sharing every detail of their lives, but to a certain extent. Jesus Himself exemplified transparency when He allowed mankind to see that He was human, He suffered, and He wept. People put some pastors' wives on a pedestal because that's what they have the tendency to act like sometime. Pastor's wives are no different; we are human, we hurt, we have emotions, and we have our bad days. If the congregation never sees us hurting, they never see us going through, they never see us having a down day, then they may view us as perfect individuals. They may also view themselves as someone who falls short, never getting to the place where nothing affects them.

For instance, I know some pastors' wives who, if they were diagnosed with cancer, they probably wouldn't tell the congregation. They may try to get the best medical care or go in their secret closets and pray and fast until God heals them. After the healing takes place, they may come out and tell it as a testimony. Well, if I can't tell it as a trial, then they don't need to hear it as a testimony. That is where the transparency comes in, being able to reveal the test and solicit the support and prayers of the congregation.

I was diagnosed with breast cancer in 1998. I didn't wait to see how it was going to pan out first. After receiving the diagnosis, I went to church the following Sunday and said to the congregation, "I've been diagnosed with breast cancer. I need you all to pray with me. For the Word of God declares in James 5:16, "Confess your faults one to another, and pray one for another, that ye may be healed. The effectual fervent prayer of a righteous man availeth much."

I don't know who the righteous man is. Who I think might be the righteous might be the biggest sinner in the church. Who I think might be the biggest sinner in the church might be the righteous one whose prayer God would hear. So, I put it out there. Saints were not only praying, they were concerned about what I needed as well. They were cooking meals, running errands, and assisting with the kids. One member was so generous as to pay for a month worth of cleaning services. When I was going through breast cancer, my favorite Scripture was Psalm 34:1: "I will bless the Lord at all times; His praise shall continually to be in my mouth." That's what got me through.

In the midst of going through breast cancer, my husband and I lost our 19-year-old son in a car accident. He just finished his first semester at the University of Kansas and was majoring in business. His desire was to obtain his degree and help his dad. While going through cancer treatments, he would sometimes drive me to do errands and to the hairdresser, as well as help out at home.

While on Christmas break from school, he obtained a job at a sporting goods store. On his first day of driving to work, he was exiting the ramp of the freeway and was hit by a fire truck. He couldn't see the fire truck because he was blindsided by an 18-wheeler truck on his left side. As he eased through the green light at the intersection, he was struck by the fire truck and killed upon impact.

My brother-in-law came and got me from the hairdresser. I said to him, "How is Markey?" He replied, "It's critical." I said, "Well, how critical is critical?" He replied, "Just come, let us go to the hospital." When we got to the hospital, the chaplain met us at the door. As pastors and pastors' wives, we know when the chaplain shows up, it is death or near death, so I knew it didn't look good.

My husband said, "Marky didn't make it." Some of our family, friends, and church members were already there, and they began to weep. I fell to my knees and said, "Oh, Lord, how could this be, how could my son be gone? How am I going to make it? I am already going through breast cancer." Immediately, the Lord brought that same Scripture back to my remembrance. He said, "But, Emelda, you said you would bless Me at all times and My praise would continually be in your mouth."

At that moment, I said, "Lord, I said it, and I will." I just began to worship the Lord in that hospital room. The nurses and doctors were looking at me like I was losing it. I continued to quote that Scripture, worshiping and praising God. I believe while I was praising God, He was healing my body of cancer and healing my mind of depression that I did not know was coming.

My son was killed on Friday, and on Sunday morning my family and I were in church praising the Lord. When you're going through something, the congregation has to be able to see that you are human, too. I was not at home, saying, "Oh, God, why did you take my son? I am already dealing with breast cancer, and now I lose my son. Lord, how could you do this? I am not going to church. I don't feel a praise."

That kind of negative talk was not going to change anything, nor was it going to help build anybody's faith, including mine. I could not go back on my promise to God. I had to move forward in spite of the hurt, pain, and grief. I had to get to church, worship God and praise my way out of that test. It was much bigger than me anyway. I believe because I honored my vow to the Lord and praised Him in the midst of it all, I am sitting here today in my right mind, free of depression and antidepressants.

My son wasn't gone but a year, and my sister was diagnosed with breast cancer. I'm being treated for breast cancer, just lost my son, and now my sister develops breast cancer. She was a single mom in California with four kids—three in the house, one grown and out of the house. I would fly out in the middle of the week every couple of months or so to California to help her. I would take her to appointments, clean her house, shop for groceries, and then cook meals to last for weeks and put in the freezer. I would fly back to Kansas City on Saturday evening and be back in church on Sunday. The congregation hardly knew I was gone.

After doing that for a year, my sister passed away, and I had to help settle her estate. When I left there, I left with an 11-year-old boy that I now had to raise. He just graduated from high school and is on his way to the University of Missouri to major in engineering.

During my nephew's junior year in high school, Hurricane Katrina hit Louisiana, and my mom lost everything she owned, with the exception of a suitcase of clothes and personal belongings. My mom was going through cancer, along with other major health challenges: diabetes, obesity, high cholesterol, and heart issues. My husband and I were in agreement that my mom could come and live with us.

Although Hurricane Katrina was horrific, it turned out to be a blessing for my mom. I became her predominant caregiver. I got her through the cancer treatment process. She's 81 and doing great. She is not only cancer free, but no longer has diabetes, high cholesterol, or heart issues, and she weighs 115 pounds. Her doctor said to me, "You have done a remarkable job taking care of your mother." Her blood work looks like that of a healthy 59-year-old woman."

God sent the healing through faith. Diet, lifestyle changes, organic supplements and good care delivered it. To God be the glory! I thank God for the knowledge He has given me and the passion to impart the knowledge into others in private, as well as corporate settings through empowerment workshops. I will be happy to share the health and wellness information that helped to restore me and my mother's health at etolbert4neolife@gmail.com.

In the course of a few years, I went through breast cancer, did all the treatments, lost my son, lost my sister to cancer, raised her son, and became the caregiver for my mother. In the midst of it all, I continued to care for my husband and family, serve faithfully as the first lady of our church, and manage my business. Nevertheless, I'm in my right mind, so I know God is still with me.

In the midst of all that you go through, you've got to have embedded in your mind and spirit that God is still faithful, and you've got to trust Him. That is not to say I didn't have some days where I thought I was going to lose my mind. Regardless of how bad some of those days got, I would continue to say, "Lord, I trust You." My daily prayer was that God would keep my mind, and He has.

I just want to say that it is not what we go through, but how we go through it. There were days I did not know how or when

I was going to get through the tests, but I knew without a doubt that God was not going to put more on me than that which I was able to bear. Whenever the negative thoughts came, I would stand firm on the vows I made to the Lord; I would bless Him at all times, and His praise would continually be in my mouth and that I trusted Him.

To this day, when someone has cancer or other major health issues, loses a child or goes through a family crisis, they call me. They may be members of our church, other local or out-of-state churches, or someone who heard my story and was encouraged by what God had done for me. God allowed me to go through all that I have been through so that He may get the glory out of my life and others may be encouraged by my testimony.

Regardless of what we go through, if we can praise him in the midst of it, He will surely bring us out of it. Don't wait until the battle is over, shout now!

CHAPTER 20

CAROLYN TRAYLOR
Widow of the Rev. Lewis Traylor, Jr.
New Israel Missionary Baptist Church
Flint, MI

"I consider it a privilege to have been able to serve in this capacity in Christian service."

Carolyn Traylor has always been active in the life of each church where she was a member. She was widowed at a young age after 24 years of marriage. She remained active in the church her husband pastored for six years after his death until she moved to Raleigh, North Carolina, and became a member at the Watts Chapel Missionary Baptist Church.

We got married in June 1972 in Baltimore. That was where I was living at the time, but he was already in Michigan. My friend Clyde and I were classmates at Spelman College. She had moved to Flint, Michigan, and she said, "Why don't you come for Christmas?" So, the first Sunday I visited her and her husband, they had Lewis over for dinner. Her husband was a pastor, and they were all friends. I was there for a week and we saw each other every day of the week.

That was December 1971. Lewis came to Maryland for my master's degree graduation ceremony at the University of Maryland—College Park. After that, we only saw each other one more time before we got married. We wrote letters every week and talked on the phone a lot. We knew God was in the plan.

I've always enjoyed church from a child up and then even in my adult life. I was very active at Knox Presbyterian Church in Baltimore. Even when I was at Spelman and we had to walk to church, I went to church every Sunday. We had chapel on Sunday afternoon and worship service every morning at 8 o'clock before class. For a couple of years, I was also the superintendent of the Sunday school at Spelman.

I have always liked church; I've always been active. It wasn't that much of a leap to marry a pastor, but I really didn't have any idea of how it was going to be. Lewis was founding pastor of New Israel. When we got married, he had been pastor for two years, and he went on to pastor for 24 more years.

The early years were what I call the "lean years" because the church basically didn't have much money. In those years, Lewis worked for General Motors and I taught school the entire time. Our things were the church's things. Lewis might go to church, call back home and say, "The light is out in the bathroom, bring a light bulb."

Back in those days, before computers and printers, I typed the bulletins on an old typewriter. He even brought one of the mimeograph duplication machines. Our resources, money, or whatever belonged to the church. I didn't mind, and my husband didn't either. As a matter of fact, we purchased the first church building in our name. My retirement money was used as collateral to get the bank loan. Then, in later years, it was taken out of our name and put into the name of the church. Those are the kinds of things that you must do to keep things going.

Anything I was asked to do, I would do it. I would get a call at 10 o'clock at night, and somebody would ask me to bring macaroni and cheese for the church dinner the next day; or maybe the program is a half hour away from starting, and I would be asked to emcee the program. Once, I was asked two weeks before Christmas to plan the Christmas program. I knew that those kinds of things happened. I did them and the Lord blessed me to do a good job.

I enjoyed our relationship with the people in our congregation. My husband was a very loving and very giving person, too. He was a strong, Christian servant, very charismatic and real friendly. He never met a stranger. He really took the needs and concerns of the people to heart.

My husband was the kind of person who would go as far as helping the members get jobs. And another thing he did—now this wasn't a good idea we found out—was loaning money. When he would do it, he would tell them don't leave the church if you find that you can't pay it back. Later, we decided that perhaps that wasn't such a good idea. I can remember giving our extra furniture to someone in need who was moving into a new apartment. Whatever we had, we shared. He wasn't just the pastor, but he was a friend, also. The members felt that they could come and talk to us about anything.

Being married to a pastor gave me a greater chance for Christian service. There is so much to be done, and I never felt overworked. Our membership wasn't that large, so I knew that meant that I would have to do many things that I wouldn't have ordinarily had to do if we had a large membership. I also wanted to support him, and I knew how deeply he felt about the church; so while being active in the church was already in me, being his wife fueled my desire to help even more. I guess being a pastor's wife led me to take things to heart more because I knew the needs and the concerns of the people, and I had a deep love for the people.

Lewis's death was "unbelievable." To this day, I still sometimes use that word *unbelievable*. He died at General Motors, having suffered a massive heart attack about one-half hour after he had gotten there. I just expected to see him back home that afternoon.

The congregation was as shocked as I was, because he wasn't sick. So, it was just a huge shock to everyone because no one expected it. It was unbelievable to me for a long, long time. But the members really rallied around me. They tried to do everything they could to help me carry on in the church because we didn't have an associate minister at that time.

When Lewis first died, every night, I sat and cried. Every night for a long time, I just sat and cried. Finally, it got to where I didn't cry every night. So then, I could tell healing was taking place. Just simple things like going past the cemetery, it got to the point where I didn't cry anymore. I could pass it without crying. It was hard, but it did get better.

I was very active with the ministers' wives group in Flint. I consider them to be my support group. When Lewis died, they really supported me during that time, helping me to get through the grieving. They called; visited; and, of course, brought food. They would write, send cards and little encouraging notes. They could empathize with what I was going through. Simple things meant so much, like following me home and seeing me inside the house after a night out at ministers' wives meeting.

We were very, very close, and I'm still in contact with a lot of them now. After Lewis died, I pretty much stopped cooking for a while, so the ministers' wives were good about inviting me out to dinner and inviting me to their homes for meals. When we had to go out of town, the wives would have me ride with them so I wouldn't have to drive.

I stayed at New Israel after Lewis died. I just wanted to do what I could to ensure that the work was carried on. And, of course, the members were extremely happy that I chose to stay after Lewis's homegoing. They counted on me for a lot. The church called a new pastor in the same year that Lewis passed.

Oftentimes, people don't know what to do with the widow, especially if you are still around. Because, who are you? You're not first lady anymore. Sometimes people don't really pay attention to the widow after the husband's gone. However, that wasn't the case at my church. I welcomed the new pastor's wife. She and I became friends in Christ. Stepping out of that role wasn't an issue for me. I knew I would never just sit in the background anyway.

As a pastor's widow, I felt loved by the congregation, but there were times that I did not feel appreciated. The only token of appreciation I received in the six years following Lewis's death was a $500 love offering one Founder's Day. As the founding pastor's wife, I felt I should have received a Christmas gift or Mother's Day present at least once. But I never received anything, and that I don't think was right. I attribute this to a lack of knowledge. I was there and just doing as much as the new pastor's wife was doing. Everything I did was in service to the Lord. It just felt like something more should have been done somewhere along the line. Eventually, when I decided to leave Michigan, I received a going-away gift from the congregation.

The church members sought my counsel on many things, and some still do. A few of us remain close. Last year, one of the members at New Israel who was in charge of Women's Day called to ask me how she should handle the Women's Day program, even down to the remarks. The sole surviving charter member of the church lives in South Carolina. I attended her husband's funeral last July. There are so many New Israel people that I have kept in touch with. It's interesting just having seen the New Israel children grow into adulthood.

After a while, I started thinking I needed a change. My daughter Kathi was moving to North Carolina and said she was not coming back. She had just graduated from college and believed there was more opportunity in Raleigh. Sadly, Flint was becoming economically depressed. Kathi wanted me to come live there since I was already spending a lot of time there after she moved. I prayed about it and finally just decided to make the move to North Carolina. It was a great decision. I joined Watts Chapel Missionary Baptist Church in Raleigh and was just as active in church there as I had always been.

I consider it a privilege to have been able to serve in this capacity in Christian service. I would do it all over again if given the chance; I wouldn't even have to think twice about it. It was also a privilege to have been able to serve and support my husband by working alongside him in all his endeavors. God has blessed me to do many things in my life, and I am still able to be of great service to my church and community.

Final Thoughts

In many contexts of the African American church collective, the first lady is expected to serve as a leader among women. The leader among women can take the shape of many forms: character, model wives and mothers, biblical knowledge, the ability to coordinate and organize, participation in ministry, a master of getting along with many people, a trendsetter, and many other things explicitly and implicitly stated. Those expectations change based on ministry contexts, on a husband's expectations, but most of all on the women who perform this role.

When we insert Shauntae, Louise, Andrea, or Judith in the role, the first lady becomes less of a church icon and more of a real woman. Just like the rest of the body of Christ, each of us brings our unique gifts, personalities, and flaws. Some women are able to slip in and out of the role with ease. For others, it is a struggle. A struggle to live up to an iconic image. A struggle to figure out what the role means for her own husband and family. A struggle of what the role means for herself. There is no one model of first lady. Some women choose to be actively involved in the life of the ministry. Others do not. Some are called to ordained ministry themselves. Others have the biblical literacy of an average church member. Some choose to be transparent with their personal lives. Others choose to protect their privacy. Because it has taken years for this manuscript to be published, time has passed. As I prefaced in the introduction, these stories are a snapshot of where the women were in a particular time in their lives. For some of them, the narrative told still holds true for them today. However, many have evolved, grown, matured from what they shared over ten years ago.

Some reactions were, "Wow, I could have handled that different-ly." Others were, "I wonder why I even cared about that then?"

Whether we would have handled situations differently, or we cared too much, or had misplaced priorities, all these experiences have shaped who we are today. The grace of God allows room for us to make mistakes, grow, be, and do better.

Whether husband, congregant, or wife, each can play a role in the journey of the woman who performs the role of pastor's wife or first lady. I encourage husbands to be sensitive to the needs and unique experiences of their wives. I encourage parishioners to give the pastor's wife freedom to be herself without judgment that she is not meeting some cultural expectation that has little biblical basis to begin with. I encourage wives to always keep their primary purpose in prominent focus, and that is to glorify God in all that we do in our thoughts, speech, and actions.

We are wives first, and every woman must figure out how to minister to her own husband. We can only glorify God and minister to our husbands when we are the woman He has created and called us to be. *The First Lady* shares the voices of 19 pastors' wives. I both encourage and challenge all first ladies, and really all women, to find their own authentic voice!

Discussion Questions

1. What should be the role of a first lady?

2. How can wives best support their husbands?

3. Is there an expectation for pastors' wives to look and act a certain way? If so, from where do those ideas come?

4. Do people put the first lady on a pedestal? How so?

5. Do first ladies expect certain treatment? Is it acceptable if she does?

6. Should a congregation honor, show appreciation to a first lady?

7. Can a congregation honor, show appreciation to a pastor but not his wife?

8. What are the explicit and implicit expectations of the pastor's wife? How does a church communicate its expectations?

9. Can a pastor's wife be friends with congregants?

10. Is there an expectation for pastor's kids (PKs) to act or be treated differently?

11. What are ways parents can ensure PKs have a healthy, balanced childhood?

12. Is it acceptable for pastors' wives to have an "inner circle" (a group of people she trusts with her children or other things) within the church?

13. What role, if any, does a husband play in establishing boundaries between the congregation and his wife and children?

14. How can a wife handle the critics of her husband?

15. How can a wife handle her own critics?

16. If a pastor's wife is also called to ministry, which role is more predominate?

17. How can a pastor's wife be exposed to the inevitable chatter (gossip, disrespect of she or husband, etc.) of church life, yet still love the people?

18. What considerations should be made in dual-career families?

19. Should pastors' wives be transparent about their personal lives?

20. Should pastors' wives be expected to participate in ministry?

21. What are the advantages and disadvantages when a pastor's wife serves in a leadership role?

22. Are there roles a pastor's wife should not perform in the life of the church?

23. How can a woman not lose herself as a pastor's wife?

24. If a pastor precedes his wife in death, how should she relate to the church? How should the church relate to her?

25. After reading this book, has the image of your first lady changed?

Participant Bios

Find out more about the women featured in
The First Lady at
www.shauntaebrownwhite.com

Additional books by the author

Communication Matters
31 Days to Speaking Life
into Your Relationships

Communication Matters
A Biblical Study for Speaking Life
into Your Relationships